MARKETING SERVICES

MARKETING SERVICES

◇◇◇◇◇◇

Competing Through Quality

Leonard L. Berry
A. Parasuraman

THE FREE PRESS
A Division of Macmillan, Inc.

NEW YORK
Maxwell Macmillan Canada
TORONTO

Maxwell Macmillan International
NEW YORK   OXFORD   SINGAPORE   SYDNEY

FREE PRESS
A Division of Simon & Schuster, Inc.
1230 Avenue of the Americas
New York, NY 10020

Designed by
Manufactured in the United States of America

10 9 8 7 6 5 4 3 2 1

Library of Congress Cataloging-In-Publication Data

Berry, Leonard L.
        Marketing services: competing through time / Leonard L. Berry, A.
        Parasuraman.
        p.   cm.
        Includes bibliographical references (p.   ) and index.
        ISBN 0-74326741-9
        1. Customer service. 2. Service industries—Marketing.
        I. Parasuraman, A. II. Title.
        HF5415.5.B48   1991
        658.8—dc20   91-13029
                                                                  CIP

For information regarding the special discounts for bulk purchases, please contact Simon ‹
Schuster Special Sales at 1-800-456-6798 or business@simonandschuster.com

*T*o a small but determined group of American and European scholars who believed marketing services was different—and built a new academic field. And to a farsighted group of service company executives who attended the early meetings, served as role models within their firms, funded the academic research, and put the research findings into practice.

To my late grandfather, Joseph Gold, who enriched my life.

—L.B.

To my sister-in-law, Sara Swamy, and her husband, Sam Swamy.

—A.P.

Contents

Acknowledgments

In this book, we bring together our combined 30-plus years of studying and writing about services marketing, contributions to the services marketing literature, and the insights of many executives and professors whom we surveyed. We aspired to write a book that would advance services marketing, a book that would build on what exists with new ideas and new wrinkles for old ideas. We wanted to write a book that not only would be interesting to read but also one that would improve the field. Hundreds of business books are published each year; we want this book to make a difference.

We are grateful to numerous people who have contributed their time, thoughts, skills, and encouragement to this volume. Chapters 2–4 are based, in part, on our ongoing research program in service quality sponsored by the Marketing Science Institute (MSI). Our co-researcher, Valarie Zeithaml of Duke University, although not an author of this book, has nonetheless made a significant contribution to it through her direct involvement in the service quality research program. We thank Professor Zeithaml for her outstanding contributions to a research program that began in 1983 and is still going strong. George Day, who recently concluded his term as Executive Director of MSI, and Katherine Jocz, Director of Research Management at MSI, have supported our research program in every possible way and we thank them both.

Adding richness to this book were the individuals who completed open-ended mail questionnaires or participated in telephone interviews concerning subject matter in which they had particular expertise. The pages that follow are filled with quotes and examples that come from this process. We are indebted to all of these accomplished people who provided such thoughtful comments.

We are also grateful to the services marketing scholars whose research we cite. The discipline of services marketing has made remarkable progress since 1977 when our friend, G. Lynn Shostack, published a landmark article in the *Journal of Marketing* entitled "Breaking Free from Product Marketing." This article stimulated the imagination of academic researchers as no other article had and fostered much of the seminal work that followed in the 1980s. To Ms. Shostack, and to other American and European researchers who gave momentum to the services marketing discipline, we tip our hats. Disciplines are built one research study, one article, one book, one conference, at a time; this book, another building block in an evolutionary process, is a tribute to many.

Finally, we thank the people who have been most closely involved in this project, living through it with us as members of the "book team":

- Glenda Bessler, our long-time administrative assistant and great friend, who performed the telephone interviewing for the book and typed every word in the manuscript.
- Shirley Bovey, an associate editor with the Real Estate Center at Texas A&M University, who moonlighted to help us edit the manuscript and who taught us to write more succinctly.
- Paul Busch, the head of Texas A&M University's Marketing Department and a wonderful friend and colleague, who has always been a strong supporter of our work.
- Robert Wallace, senior editor at The Free Press, who has now worked with us on two books, and has been very helpful on both.
- Our families, who have understood that we were occupied with a project of considerable personal importance.

LEONARD L. BERRY
A. PARASURAMAN

Authors' Note

A number of individuals provided original material for this book by contributing written statements or participating in telephone interviews. Individuals who are quoted without an accompanying citation participated in our mail and telephone surveys. All quotations are used with permission.

An Integrative Framework for Marketing Services

1

◇◇◇

Services and Quality

A guest at the Holiday Inn on Union Square in San Francisco is attempting to turn on the radio in his room. No matter which button he pushes the radio will not play. Finally, the guest reports a defective radio. A hotel employee soon arrives at the guest's room with a new radio, a box of chocolates, and flowers. As for the radio already in the room, the employee turns it on without difficulty (it plays perfectly) and quickly reassures the guest that the radio is tricky to operate. The server shows the guest how to work the radio and pleasantly exits the room, leaving both radios, the chocolates, and the flowers.

An elderly woman is in her favorite food store, Ukrop's Super Markets of Richmond, Virginia. She picks up a large pineapple from the display case, holds it for several moments, and then returns it with obvious reluctance. Ukrop's president, James Ukrop, witnesses this scene and asks the customer if she would like to buy half of the pineapple, indicating that the store would be glad to cut it in half. The customer accepts and states how she looks forward to visiting Ukrop's because the staff is so friendly and makes her feel so welcome.

The manager of the downtown Chicago Marriott hotel discovers that two thirds of all guest calls to housekeeping are requests for ironing boards. This discovery leads to the idea of placing irons and ironing boards in each guest room. The problem is where to find the $20,000 this will cost. The hotel manager reviews the capital budget and notes that $22,000 is earmarked to replace black-and-white television sets with color sets in the bathrooms of concierge-level guest rooms. The manager inquires how many VIP guests have requested color television sets for their bathrooms and learns that no guest has ever made such a request. So the manager cancels plans to buy color sets and adds the irons and ironing boards. The result is no net addition to the capital budget, a big productivity boost for housekeeping, and an important new guest room feature.

Night after night, Aurora, Colorado, police officers answer calls for break-ins of cars parked outside a local dance hall. One officer notes that the burglaries usually involve purses and interviews female customers who say they lock their handbags in their parked cars, fearing the bags would be stolen from unattended tables during dances. The officer then persuades the dance hall owner to install lockers and the burglary calls drop from dozens each month to two in four months.[1]

These four stories underscore our central argument in this book: *the essence of services marketing is service.* Service quality is the foundation of services marketing. The textbooks stress the four Ps of marketing—product, place, promotion, and price—but in a service business none of this works very well without a Q—for quality.

The stories illustrate that cutting-edge services marketing is less the slick and fancy and more old-fashioned virtues such as caring and common sense. They illustrate the marketing power of doing the little things that competitors forget to do, from delivering flowers and chocolates with a radio to placing irons and ironing boards in the closets of hotel rooms. They illustrate the importance of customer-friendly service designs, such as outfitting a dance hall with lockers. Finally, the stories illustrate that everyone performing a service is a marketer, from a supermarket president who roams the store aisles to a hotel housekeeper who teaches guests how to operate a (poorly designed) radio.

Effective services marketing is a strong service concept delivered well, a desired service performed excellently. This synergy of strategy *and* execution fuels service industry builders and leaders, from Domino's Pizza to Cable News Network (CNN), from Federal Express to Walt Disney World, from ServiceMaster to Southwest Airlines. Each of these industry leaders reflects a special chemistry that combines a big idea and superior execution.

The big idea alone offers only a temporary advantage. Companies that pioneer successful new service concepts always face ambitious competitors unashamed to imitate. Pizza Hut had little choice but to add home-delivery service given the dynamic growth of Domino's. Federal Express's success ushered in a horde of new competitors—and a climate of fierce price-cutting—in the overnight mail business.

Superior execution is vital to *sustaining* the success initiated by an innovative service concept. An innovator's service quality is usually more difficult to imitate than its service concept. This is because quality service comes from inspired leadership throughout an organization, a customer-minded corporate culture, excellent service-system design, the effective use of information and technology, and other factors that develop slowly in a company, if at all. Entering the home-delivery pizza business is one matter. Performing this service as well as Domino's Pizza is quite another matter.

Service quality is the foundation for services marketing because the core product being marketed is a performance. The performance *is* the product; the performance is what customers buy. A strong service concept gives companies the opportunity to compete for customers; a strong performance of the service concept builds competitiveness by earning customers' confidence and reinforcing branding, advertising, selling, and pricing.

SERVICES MARKETING VERSUS GOODS MARKETING

In manufacturing, the marketing function plays (or should play) a dominant role in customer need identification and product development prior to production and in effecting product demand following production. Production precedes demand stimulation, which precedes consumption. Marketing's post-production roles include creating brand awareness, inducing brand trial, demonstrating brand benefits, and building brand preference. Customers assess the brand's promised benefits during consumption, strengthening or weakening brand preference accordingly.

The chronological sequence of the four functional phases are shown in Exhibit 1–1. It also delineates the contributions of post-production marketing, consumption, and word-of-mouth communications—spawned by other customers' experiences with the brand—to brand awareness, trial, demonstration, and preference. The tangibility of goods and their visible demonstration enable the marketing department to perform effectively all four demand-stimulation roles *prior to a customer's purchase commitment*. Likewise, product tan-

Exhibit 1–1 Nature and Roles of Goods Marketing

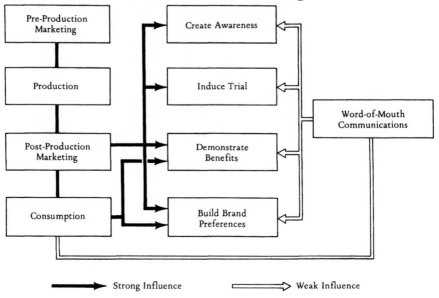

Strong Influence → Weak Influence

gibility can boost prospective customers' confidence in their own evaluation of goods, thereby lowering their reliance on word-of-mouth communications.

The limited promotional impact of word-of-mouth communications is signified by the thin-line arrows in Exhibit 1–1. When word-of-mouth communications do exert a strong influence on the purchase of goods—automobiles and personal computers, for example—it is usually because customers perceive difficulty in evaluating the product prior to purchase and perceive risk in making a mistake. In general, the more difficult it is for customers to evaluate salient aspects of a product prior to purchase, the stronger the potential influence of word-of-mouth communications and the more the product will need to be marketed like a service.

As Exhibit 1–2 shows, the nature and roles of marketing differ for services. Although both services marketing and goods marketing start with the critical need-identification and product design functions, goods generally are produced before sold and services generally are sold before produced. Moreover, services marketing has a more limited influence on customers prior to purchase than goods marketing. Whereas goods marketers may be able to move prospective customers from brand awareness to brand preference with pack-

Exhibit 1-2 Nature and Roles of Services Marketing

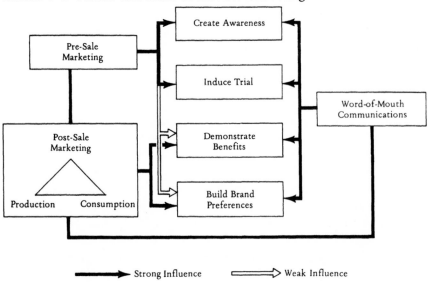

aging, promotion, pricing, and distribution, services marketers usually cannot.

Customers must experience the intangible service to really know it. Intangibility makes services more difficult for customers to imagine and desire than goods. Customers purchasing professional tax advice have no knobs to turn, buttons to push, or pictures to see. Customers' perception of risk tends to be high for services because services cannot be touched, smelled, tasted, or tried on before purchase. Customers can test-drive a new automobile and kick the tires, but to try a new vacation resort they must first register as guests.[2]

Services are dominated by experience qualities, attributes that can be meaningfully evaluated only after purchase and during production-consumption.[3] In services, both *post-sale marketing* through orchestrating a satisfying experience for customers during production and *word-of-mouth communication* (which is surrogate and supplement for customers' direct experiences) have prominent effects in winning customers' loyalty. Exhibit 1-2 shows these relatively strong influences. Services marketers can create brand awareness and induce trial before the sale, but they demonstrate benefits and build brand preference most effectively after the sale.

Superior service cannot be manufactured in a factory, packaged, and delivered intact to customers. Instead, for many services customers actually enter the "factory" (the airport and airplane, for example) to consume the service as it is produced. The "producers" with whom customers interact, such as airline ticket agents, flight attendants, and baggage handlers, perform the dual role of "marketers." How service personnel conduct themselves in the customers' presence—how they act, what they say, what they don't say, their overall appearance—influences whether customers buy from the firm again.

If a worker in an appliance factory has an aloof attitude, is poorly dressed, or has body odor, the consumer will never know it because producer and consumer never meet. However, if a medical doctor has an aloof attitude, a restaurant waiter an unkempt appearance, or a taxi driver body odor, customer perceptions of the service are affected profoundly. A service company that does relatively little pre-sale marketing but is truly dedicated to delivering excellent quality service will enjoy greater marketing effectiveness—higher customer retention, more sales to existing customers, greater success at converting prospects to customers through positive word-of-mouth communications—than a company emphasizing pre-sale marketing but falling short during actual service delivery.

SERVICES IN MANUFACTURING

Although comparing the nature and roles of goods and services marketing is useful, an easy dichotomy between manufacturing and service firms does not exist. In reality, service output is a major, if not *the* major, success factor for manufacturing companies.

One force pushing manufacturers toward more service-intensive operations is the greater potential for building sustainable competitive advantage through service rather than goods. Quinn, Doorley, and Paquette state the point well:

> True strategic focus means that a company can concentrate more power in its chosen markets than anyone else can. Once this meant owning the largest resource base, manufacturing plants, research labs, or distribution channels to support product lines. Now physical facilities—including a seemingly superior product—seldom provide a sustainable competitive edge. They are too easily bypassed, reverse engineered, cloned, or slightly surpassed. Instead, a maintainable advantage usually

derives from outstanding depth in selected human skills, logistics capabilities, knowledge bases, or other service strengths that competitors cannot reproduce and that lead to greater demonstrable value for the customer.[4]

Smart manufacturing company executives are as interested in service quality as goods quality, in selling the intangibles as the tangibles, in entering new markets for services as entering new markets for goods. They recognize that the core benefit their customers buy is delivered not by a good or a service but by both. They view the synergy of tangible and intangible as the value-adding, differentiating output.

Manufacturers are service firms too, just less so than companies commonly considered to be service firms. If the source of a product's core benefit is more tangible than intangible, it would be considered a good. If the core benefit source is more intangible than tangible, it would be considered a service. However, virtually all products have both tangible and intangible elements that contribute to the core benefit, as Exhibit 1–3 shows. Value-conscious automobile buyers do not just buy the car; they buy a system of transportation that will give them their money's worth. Thus, a dealer's reputation for professional sales and service, spare parts availability, warranty protection, and other factors influence the selection of make and model.

Most companies operate within the dotted lines in Exhibit 1–3. And those firms now outside these lines may well move toward them

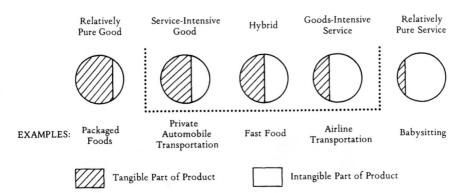

Exhibit 1–3 The Goods-Service Spectrum

SOURCE: The conceptualization of this exhibit was inspired by G. Lynn Shostack, "Breaking Free from Product Marketing," *Journal of Marketing,* April 1977, pp. 73–80.

in an effort to add value to and differentiate their products. A packaged food company, for example, might add toll-free telephone lines to provide information for customers, sponsor cooking schools, and offer recipe services. A babysitting service might take electronic games to the home for the children to enjoy.

In this book, we use the terms *services marketing* and *goods marketing* because there are differences. And we refer to service companies and to manufacturers because most companies are more one than the other. But we do submit that the lines of distinction between the manufacturing and service sectors are blurring and that the arena of consequence within manufacturing will increasingly be service.

AN INTEGRATIVE FRAMEWORK

We have written this book to present service quality and services marketing as one discipline. These are not separate disciplines or even allied disciplines. Rather, one (service quality) is a subset of the other (services marketing). In this book, we strive to capture in an integrated framework salient concepts of services marketing—the concepts that matter most when the product is a performance—and we attempt to take these ideas further than they have been taken before. Exhibit 1–4 presents the services marketing framework that we develop in this book. Chapters 2–4 concern the service quality

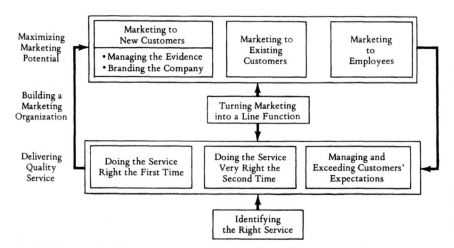

Exhibit *1–4* An Integrative Framework for Marketing Services

foundation: service reliability ("Doing the Service Right the First Time"), service recovery ("Doing the Service Very Right the Second Time"), and strong interactive service ("Managing and Exceeding Customers' Expectations"). These chapters are based in part on research we have conducted since finishing our earlier book, *Delivering Quality Service*,[5] written with our colleague, Valarie Zeithaml.

Chapter 5 ("Turning Marketing into a Line Function") concerns the primary roles of the marketing department in building a services marketing organization. Special emphasis is placed on creating marketing energy in the line organization closest to end-customers. Developing marketing skills and a customer-minded attitude among line employees helps a service company improve its service and maximize its marketing potential. In services, it is line employees who deliver the service promised or don't, cross-sell the service line or simply take orders, build the company's brand image or destroy it.

Chapter 6 ("Managing the Evidence") concerns turning tangibles in the service environment to advantage and Chapter 7 ("Branding the Company") concerns transforming the company itself into a powerful message. The intangibility of services makes evidence management and branding critical to services marketing success. New customers in particular are attentive to clues about the service because they have little or no other experience with the company on which to base their initial impressions. Hence, we place evidence management and branding in the marketing-to-new-customer box in our model, while making it quite clear in the chapters that the ideas also apply beyond new customer marketing.

Chapter 8 ("Marketing to Existing Customers") emphasizes the superior profit opportunities with current customers and discusses success factors in relationship marketing. Chapter 9 ("Marketing to Employees") presents the concept of employees as customers and discusses the success factors in internal marketing. Chapter 10 ("Services Marketing in the Nineties") reflects on how services marketing will be changing.

As our model suggests, services marketers must be effective with each customer type: new, existing, and internal. Service companies must first attract new customers if they are to build customer relationships. Firms must market to employees because they are the performers and the performance is the product. The model's arrows show the cross-influences at work in services marketing. Delivering quality service stimulates favorable word-of-mouth communications and helps a company attract more new customers, results in more satisfied existing customers, and provides a more fulfilling and rewarding work environment for internal customers. Conversely, firms that effectively manage evidence and branding, build customer relationships, and market internally will improve service in the process. The marketing department, in the middle of the model, builds a strong marketing organization by focusing its energies and resources on service improvement in particular, and on creating value for new, existing, and internal customers in general.

II

◇◇◇◇

Quality:
The Foundation
for Services Marketing

2

◇◇◇

Doing the Service
Right the First Time

S ervice reliability—*performing the service dependably and accurately*—is the heart of services marketing excellence. When a
company performs a service carelessly, when it makes avoidable mistakes, when it fails to deliver on alluring promises made to attract
customers, it shakes the customers' confidence in its capabilities and
undermines its chances of earning a reputation for service excellence.
From the customer's perspective, the proof of a service is its flawless
performance.

RELIABILITY IS PARAMOUNT

Common sense underscores the importance of reliability in delivering quality service. Who wants to travel on an airline whose pilots
are *usually* dependable, be operated on by a surgeon who *usually*
remembers where on the body the surgery is to be done, or bank with
a financial institution that *usually* keeps accurate records? When we
have our customer hats on, "usually" isn't good enough. And it is
not just the "high-stake" services involving our health or financial
security for which we demand reliability. The dry cleaner that loses
our shirts, the automobile repair firm that says our car is fixed when
it isn't, the taxi service that forgets to pick us up to go to the airport—these service providers also lose our confidence. And our business.

That reliability is paramount to service customers is strongly supported by findings from formal research studies. Since 1983 we have been systematically investigating the topic of service quality through a series of studies in sectors ranging from "pure" services (e.g., insurance) to services associated with tangible products (e.g., appliance repair).[1] Empirical evidence from our research consistently shows that reliability is the foremost criterion customers consider in evaluating a company's quality of service.

To be sure, reliability is not the sole determinant of customers' service-quality evaluations. Our research suggests five general dimensions that influence customers' assessments of service quality:

Reliability:	The ability to perform the promised service dependably and accurately.
Tangibles:	The appearance of physical facilities, equipment, personnel, and communications materials.
Responsiveness:	The willingness to help customers and to provide prompt service.
Assurance:	The knowledge and courtesy of employees and their ability to convey trust and confidence.
Empathy:	The provision of caring, individualized attention to customers.

Reliability, however, has repeatedly emerged as the most critical dimension in every study in which we have measured the relative importance of the five dimensions (to date we have completed ten such studies involving independent customer samples). In our latest set of studies, we asked more than 1,900 customers of five different service companies to rate the relative importance of the five dimensions by allocating 100 points among them. The point allocations imply the following rank-order (average points allocated shown in parentheses): reliability (32), responsiveness (22), assurance (19), empathy (16), and tangibles (11). Reliability is the essence of service quality which, in turn, is the basis for services marketing excellence. Thus, as Exhibit 2–1 shows, service reliability is the very core of services marketing excellence.

BENEFITS OF SERVICE RELIABILITY

Performing the service right the first time contributes significantly to a company's profits by simultaneously improving marketing effec-

Exhibit 2-1 The Foundation for Services Marketing Excellence

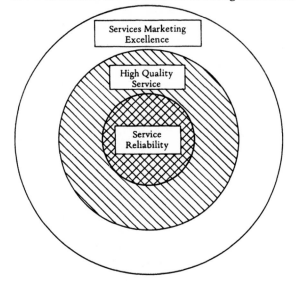

tiveness and operating efficiency. Exhibit 2–2 summarizes the ways improved service reliability can boost a company's bottom line.

Our studies of large, well-known U.S. companies consistently show that customers perceive them to be more deficient in reliability than in any other dimension. Given the prevalence of service errors and broken service promises, consistent reliability gives a company the opportunity to compete effectively and build a reputation for service. Achieving competitive differentiation through consistent service reliability can provide several significant marketing benefits: higher current-customer retention rates (and reduced pressure to engage in expensive efforts to recruit new customers), more business from current customers,[2] increased word-of-mouth communications promoting the company, and greater opportunity for commanding a premium price.

In numerous customer focus groups that we have conducted as part of our programmatic research on service quality, participants frequently have bemoaned the paucity of dependable service and expressed their willingness to reward handsomely reliable service companies. An appliance-repair service customer illustrates: "I do not mind paying even $50 or $60 a service call *if* I can find a repairperson who shows up on time and does the job right. . . . I will not even

Exhibit 2–2 Potential Benefits of Service Reliability

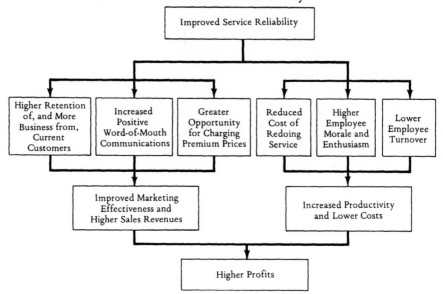

consider shopping around if I can find such a person." A recent *Wall Street Journal*/NBC News survey confirms customers' willingness to pay a premium for superior service. Thirty-five percent of the survey respondents said most of the time they buy from companies that charge higher prices but provide better service. An additional 40 percent said they do so at least some of the time.[3]

Clever commercials, eye-catching advertisements, and other promotional inducements will be ineffective without reliable service. Indeed, such marketing strategies will do more harm than good when firms promise more than they deliver.

Service reliability also contributes to operating efficiencies by reducing the need for reperforming the service. However, the cost of unreliable service includes not only the direct expense of redoing the service but also the indirect penalties associated with the negative publicity generated by displeased customers. Thus, the total cost of correcting the damage done by a defective service and hence the potential saving from doing the service right the first time can be substantial. A surgeon who leaves a surgical tool inside a patient's body, a car mechanic who replaces a properly functioning part instead of the defective one, a stock broker who buys 1,000 shares when the client's instructions are to *sell* 1,000 shares, or a hotel that has no accommodation for a customer holding a confirmed reservation will pay a hefty price for faulty service.

The interaction between service employees and customers that accompanies the production and consumption of many services implies additional, albeit less apparent, ways service reliability can contribute to productivity gains and cost savings. The morale, job satisfaction, and job commitment of front-line service employees are inversely related to the frustration levels of customers they deal with day after day. Interacting with frustrated customers demanding explanations and restitution for defective services can demoralize employees, deflate their enthusiasm for their jobs, and decrease their commitment to their companies.

Companies suffering from chronic service unreliability—an airline that is usually late and frequently cancels flights, an equipment repair company that does not provide its technicians with the requisite training and tools for accurately diagnosing equipment problems— are at tremendous risk of being trapped into a vicious spiral of declining employee morale, deteriorating service performance, increasing employee turnover, falling productivity, and escalating costs. In contrast, companies that place a premium on service reliability, institute incentives to encourage it, and possess the resources to achieve it foster a positive work environment that engenders higher productivity and lower costs by enhancing employee morale, enthusiasm, and commitment.

We sometimes hear executives say that 98 percent reliability is acceptable and that it is cost-prohibitive to do better. We disagree. The flip side of 98 percent reliability is 2 percent unreliability, and the total cost of 2 percent unreliability will almost always be higher than the cost of improving.

In their recent book, *Service Breakthroughs,* Professors James Heskett, Earl Sasser, and Christopher Hart distinguish between "merely good" service managers and "breakthrough" service managers. They describe the differing attitudes of the two groups toward improving service reliability. "Merely good" service managers believe in an "optimal" level of defect-free service beyond which it is uneconomical to improve reliability. In contrast, "breakthrough" service managers pursue the goal of 100 percent defect-free ser "merely good" managers seriously considered the myriac and operating benefits of improved service reliability, the alize that striving for 100 percent reliability is a potentia pursuit. Aiming for any lower target will be tantamount themselves—and their companies—to the title of "also rans" while more enlightened competitors pass them by.

DELIVERING RELIABLE SERVICE

Building and nurturing a "zero defects" culture is as critical in services as in manufacturing. However, the goal of zero defects is more complex in services for several reasons. First, the decoupling of production and consumption of goods provides manufacturers with the opportunity to weed out defective products before they get to customers. A goods manufacturer can deliver defect-free products even when in-the-factory reliability is less than 100 percent. In contrast, for most services in-the-factory reliability is inseparable from in-the-field reliability because *the field is the factory.* Service flaws such as a repairperson's failure to show up at the scheduled time or a restaurant's failure to have a reserved table ready as promised occur in the customer's presence. Thus, performing a service right the first time involves a greater sense of immediacy and requires a greater degree of discipline than ensuring a good is defect-free when a customer gets it.

Second, service intangibility implies that criteria for flawless services are less concrete and more subjective than criteria for defect-free tangible products. The reliability of microchips or motorcycles can be assessed more objectively—based on more precise criteria accepted by both producers and customers—than the accuracy of medical diagnoses or investment advice. For these and many other services, customers' perceptions of whether the services are performed correctly are the prime determinants of their reliability. Even when a service meets provider-established criteria for correct execution, it is not error free unless it also meets customers' criteria, regardless of how subjective or nebulous those criteria are. For instance, patients might assess the accuracy of their physician's diagnoses on the basis of time spent examining them, even though examination time, by itself, may be technically unimportant. Customers' expectations and requirements are the *real* reliability standards when that being evaluated is essentially a performance rather than an object.

Third, the term "defect" has a broader meaning in services than in manufacturing. Specifically, an otherwise accurate service still should be considered flawed if it confuses or frustrates customers.

Customer confusion and frustration can flood a company with inquiries and complaints, and hence adversely affect marketing effectiveness and operating efficiency. Confusing services (e.g., computerized home-banking services that customers cannot comprehend easily), or confusing *service components* of goods (e.g., improper installation instructions accompanying home appliances), are flawed. The productivity losses they engender in provider organizations are akin to discarded defectives—"scrap"—in the manufacturing sector.

Clearly, the complexity of service reliability poses unique challenges to companies striving for zero service defects. These challenges include delivering error-free service in *real time*, ascertaining and understanding customers' subjective standards (the true yardsticks for assessing service reliability), and recognizing that unclear, confusing services are subtle but significant contributors to service "scrap."

Effectively tackling these challenges requires various activities aimed at avoiding service failures. These activities fall under three broad categories: (1) providing service leadership; (2) thoroughly testing and retesting services; and (3) building and nurturing an organizational *infrastructure* for error-free service.

As depicted in Exhibit 2–3, the three sets of activities constitute vital, interlinked pillars of support for service reliability. We now examine in detail the composition of each pillar and its role in improving service reliability.

SERVICE LEADERSHIP

Strong leaders with a passion for perfection are the lifeblood of a reliability-centered service strategy. Leaders who set high service standards nurture a "do-it-right-first" culture. Companies achieve renown for service reliability through senior executives who:

- Firmly believe that 100 percent reliability is a feasible and worthwhile goal
- Frequently and effectively communicate their belief companywide
- Reward error-free service
- Are never content with the status quo and strive for continuous improvement

Exhibit 2–3 Three Pillars of Support for Service Reliability

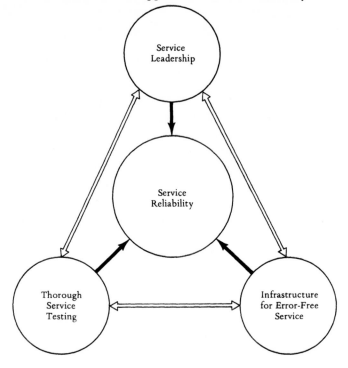

Will Potter, CEO of Maryland-based Preston Trucking Company, recently selected as one of the ten best companies to work for in the United States, emphasizes his commitment to reliable service by having each employee sign the Company's Commitment to Excellence statement. The statement, posted in each Preston facility, reads in part:

> Once I make a commitment to a customer or another associate, I promise to fulfill it on time. I will do what I say when I say I will do it. . . . I understand that one claim or one mistake is one error too many. I promise to do my job right the first time and to continually seek improvement.[5]

The enduring commitment to the pursuit of 100 percent reliability exemplified by Will Potter is echoed by leaders of other companies with well-known reputations for excellence. James Houghton, Chairman and CEO of Corning, Inc., emphasizes the need for continuous service improvement: "Instead of ending, a quality learning curve keeps charting new territory. It continues to focus activity on customer requirements, employee empowerment, reduced variation and zero errors. It makes high quality plus low-cost production a reality. Goals, no longer ends in themselves, become directional signs to ever higher goals."[6]

Jack Roberts, Vice President for Quality at Federal Express, also sounds the bell of continuous improvement: "We are delivering 1,250,000 packages a day. If we have a 99 percent success rate that [still] means we have thousands of customers a day that are unhappy with us. That is unacceptable. Our objective is to drive down the absolute number of failures."[7]

Management's focus on the *absolute number* of failures—rather than on the less stringent criterion of failures expressed as a percentage—epitomizes the culture of continuous improvement found in companies that deliver world-class quality. Strong leaders who champion flawless service foster the attitude "If it isn't fixed, it will break" instead of the attitude "If it isn't broken, don't fix it." Thus, the service-leadership pillar reinforces a second pillar of service reliability—thorough service testing.

THOROUGH SERVICE TESTING

Premature market introduction of a service prior to rigorous testing is a primary cause of service unreliability. The service sector frequently fails to subject new services to the same level of scrutiny that new manufactured products undergo. Research and testing during new-service design to identify and eliminate potential flaws is more the exception than the rule.

Service intangibility is a key reason for inadequate testing and hasty launching of new services. Because services lack the concreteness of physical goods, the temptation to bypass pre-launch testing is powerful. The challenges of conducting consumer research and performing product tests on abstract service concepts may appear daunting to many service companies. Nevertheless, they must accept and effectively tackle these challenges if zero errors is their goal.

Service marketers can and should expose new service concepts to rigorous customer and line employee feedback, carefully examine the service design and delivery process before introduction to identify potential glitches, and whenever possible introduce the new service in limited distribution to allow additional fine-tuning before a full-scale launch. As Lynn Shostack, President of Joyce International Inc., puts it: "There is simply no substitute for a proper rehearsal."[8]

Pre-launch Testing. Citibank has one of the most successful automatic teller machine (ATM) programs of any bank in America, but not by accident. For years Citibank has tested new service concepts in a mock banking facility known as "the lab." By 1977, when Citibank implemented its decision to cover New York City with ATMs, the machine had been through six iterative cycles of testing and improvement in the lab. Questioning and observing customers in the lab helped Citibank develop a state-of-the-art technology for its time.

Since introducing its first ATMs, Citibank has continued to use the lab to develop a new generation of ATMs now installed in New York—more than 1,200 of them. The new ATMs have several user-friendly features such as colorful graphics and a touch screen instead of a keyboard. The machines function in English, Spanish, and Chinese, with other languages to be added.[9]

Citibank's patient, thorough approach to the ATM service contrasts sharply with Federal Express's ill-fated adventure with Zap-Mail, an electronic document transmission service that was withdrawn in September 1986 with a $190 million after-tax write-off. The promise of ZapMail was the delivery of high quality document copies anywhere in the United States within two hours through facsimile transmission and courier service. The reality of ZapMail was an unreliable service resulting from light originals that wouldn't reprint, broken facsimile machines, and telephone line disturbances.

In launching the ZapMail service, Federal Express made the fatal error of failing to anticipate the process snafus that thorough pre-launch testing—"proper rehearsal" in Shostack's words—would have brought to its attention. Of course, rapid improvements in facsimile technology coupled with declining costs compounded ZapMail's woes as the best prospects for electronic document transmission found they could do for themselves more conveniently and inexpensively the service Federal Express wanted to perform for them. Thus, Federal Express eventually would have had a tough go with ZapMail even if it had solved the technical problems prior to introduction. However, by rushing to market a service riddled with potential problems—by starting weak—Federal Express had no chance for even temporary success with ZapMail.[10]

Service Blueprinting. A powerful technique for recognizing and rectifying service "fail points"—the elements of the service most prone to problems—is *service blueprinting*, "a way of diagramming and describing the total system and total concept to ensure that all issues and areas are addressed that are necessary to the successful development of a service."[11] A service blueprint is a planning and diagnostic document that depicts the service events and processes in a flow chart. It gives meaning and structure to an otherwise intangible abstraction. As such, the blueprint is a tool for systematically evaluating the service to identify and prepare for potential problems that might ordinarily escape detection. The Richmond Metropolitan Blood Service, a nonprofit regional blood bank, recently blueprinted its mobile blood-drive system that generates more than 70 percent of the blood it collects each year. The blueprint revealed 28 potential fail points and served as the basis for training sessions to teach employees how to prevent such failures and how to handle them if they do occur.[12]

Lynn Shostack, who pioneered the concept of service blueprinting, summarizes its benefits: "A service blueprint allows a company to test its assumptions on paper and thoroughly work out the bugs; a service manager can test the prototype delivery on customers and use the feedback to modify the blueprint before testing the procedure again. The alternative—leaving services to individual talent and managing the pieces rather than the whole—makes a company more vulnerable and creates a service that reacts slowly to market opportunities."[13]

Post-launch Testing. Rigorous pre-launch testing alone is not sufficient for pursuing zero defects in services. Also needed is regular and systematic reevaluation of the service after introduction to detect, correct, and learn from fail points that may not have emerged during earlier testing. In sharp contrast to goods, services—especially those requiring a great deal of human input—are *heterogeneous:* their nature and performance can vary from provider to provider, from customer to customer, from day to day.[14] Therefore even a comprehensive pre-launch test and rehearsal may not reveal everything that could go wrong.

Conducting service-quality research on an ongoing basis is one approach for quickly sensing service shortfalls and eliminating them. Employing "mystery shoppers"—researchers posing as customers to experience and evaluate the service firsthand—and performing periodic customer surveys are especially effective techniques for uncovering trouble spots.

A complementary approach for improving service reliability is to solicit input from employees actually performing the service.

Customer-contact personnel, by virtue of being integral to the service delivery process, have an excellent vantage point for observing the service and suggesting better ways to perform it. Unfortunately, many service companies have no mechanism for effectively tapping this rich source of service-improvement ideas. They have not established the communication channels, inducements, and reward systems to capture and act on suggestions of front-line employees. Companies with their sights trained on zero service errors can ill afford to ignore the wealth of reliability-improvement ideas that may be buried in their own backyards—or *frontyards.*

Fidelity Bank in Philadelphia has created a formal system, called FAST FORWARD, for capitalizing on employee ideas and suggestions. The job descriptions of all employees in the bank's Centralized Customer Service Center include problem prevention as a primary responsibility. These employees fill out FAST FORWARD forms whenever customers report problems that the employees believe could have been avoided. The FAST FORWARD forms become part of the employees' records and are used in appraising their performance. Employees can earn a bonus of up to $300 per month depending on how valuable their suggestions are.[15] Says Jane Marie Nigro, Customer Service Operations Officer: "The FAST FORWARD program reinforces management's desire to listen and respond to employee ideas. When the staff is asked how to better serve customers, the results are unbelievable. Everyone has suggestions worth listening to and FAST FORWARD provides a superb forum."

Systematic, in-depth analysis of customer complaints and inquiries is yet another source of information for reassessing and refining a service to enhance reliability and improve process efficiency. American Express excels at performing such an analysis and acting on the findings. Using an approach it calls "avoidable input analysis," American Express continuously strives to eliminate unnecessary customer inquiries stemming from billing disputes, unclear marketing programs, and other service shortfalls. It analyzes 147 different types of customer phone calls to root out the causes of problem calls and to reduce unnecessary customer input.[16]

Through its "avoidable input analysis," American Express derives a double benefit: its services are more dependable from the customer's standpoint and its productivity is higher as a result of reduced "scrap." MaryAnn Rasmussen, Vice President of Worldwide Quality at American Express, illustrates this benefit with a recent application of avoidable input analysis: "With the [customer-inquiry] tracking system we have in place, we learned that we were receiving many inquiries related to purchases made by cardmembers overseas. We realized that we could significantly reduce the number of these inquiries by educating cardmembers in the cultural and legal differences in making purchases abroad. We addressed this educational need by developing a guide for our most frequent travelers. This booklet is good for cardmembers because it helps them make wiser purchasing decisions, and it's good for us because it reduces our most expensive inquiries to research."

INFRASTRUCTURE FOR ERROR-FREE SERVICE

The two supportive pillars of service reliability discussed so far—service leadership and thorough service testing—are linked to and buttressed by a third pillar: infrastructure for error-free service. We use the term "infrastructure" to capture the myriad organizational factors that should be in place to sustain a "do-it-right-first" culture. Virtually all these factors concern personnel and teamwork issues.

Personnel. Company personnel responsible for performing services are a critical ingredient of the infrastructure for defect-free service. Most service businesses are people-intensive, with employee-customer interactions a significant part of the services delivered. Virtually every employee in a service company interacts with and serves either external customers or internal customers (i.e., other employees). Moreover, the quality of service received by internal customers strongly influences the quality of service extended to external customers.[17] Therefore, the performance of all employees, regardless of the customer types they serve, ultimately influences external customers' assessments of the delivered service. Employee attitudes and behavior can erode or enhance a company's service reputation.

David B. Luther, Senior Vice President and Corporate Director of Quality, Corning, Inc., strongly believes in the crucial role of customer service in providing a competitive edge to goods manufacturers. He identifies the following employee perceptions and attitudes as key barriers to progress toward zero errors:[18]

- I do not *want* to improve quality
- I am not *expected* to improve quality

- I am not *able* to improve quality

To achieve progress toward error-free service, employees must be willing and capable; management must encourage these traits. Ensuring that employees possess these necessary traits is a challenge. Executives can meet this challenge effectively by hiring the best-qualified people for the service roles; teaching the why and how of service reliability in training programs; setting reliability standards and measuring performance against them; instituting visible and meaningful rewards for error-free service; and continually emphasizing the importance of reliability in company communications, including missions statements. These strategies coupled with inspiring leadership by service-reliability champions will produce a force powerful enough to eliminate the barriers that Dave Luther talks about.

Teamwork. Effective teamwork among employees and interfunctional communications also are crucial components of an infrastructure for error-free service. The lack of interdepartmental understanding, cooperation, and communication contributes significantly to unreliable service. Many service companies are organized along strict functional lines, presumably to streamline operations and increase efficiency. Unfortunately, this within-function focus erects barriers rather than bridges between departments. As a result, the service "parts" produced by the different functions often do not dovetail to produce a reliable service that reassures customers they are dealing with a unified company.

Our research shows that the lack of interfunctional coordination and communication, in addition to frustrating customers with undependable service, also frustrates employees and adversely affects their performance.

We recently completed an in-depth study of a large industrial services company that performs a number of services for client firms and their employees on a contract basis. The company's services are complex, involving many potential fail points resulting from the need for input from and coordination among multiple functions and frequent contacts with a variety of personnel in client firms. Consequently, although this company is the leader in its industry and perceived as such by the marketplace, it suffers from serious internal vulnerabilities capable of tarnishing its reputation. In diagnosing the causes underlying these vulnerabilities, the lack of interdepartmental synergy emerged as a prime suspect regardless of which part of the company we examined. The following employee comments from three separate focus groups illustrate:

- Everyone should understand why they are doing what they are doing and how their jobs tie in with those of others. I think we can do a better job of internal communication.
- It is amazing. . . . We are all working under the same roof but you don't have any idea what others are doing.
- My biggest problem is getting answers from other departments in a timely fashion.

Inadequate communication between customer-contact personnel who perform the service and personnel who promote the service is a particularly pervasive—and direct—cause of service unreliability. Service promisers (e.g., advertising and sales personnel) who make commitments to customers before discussing with service providers the feasibility of meeting those commitments, and service providers who are unaware of the commitments made to customers, contribute to a cycle of service-promise breaking. In the course of our research we have seen much evidence of overpromising and broken promises because service promisers and providers do not work as a team.

Fostering teamwork among service employees requires some degree of structuring, assigning, and facilitating by management, especially in companies with entrenched functional boundaries and fears about "losing turf." But the payoff from replacing or supplementing a traditional functional structure with interfunctional, customer-focused teams will be substantial, both in terms of fulfilling customer requirements *and* fostering employee productivity.

Lakeland Regional Medical Center, an 897-bed hospital in Lakeland, Florida, is one of an increasing number of service organizations that are creatively applying the team concept and are reaping handsome returns as a result. Each Lakeland patient in a 40-bed pilot unit is assigned a "care pair"—usually a registered nurse and a helper—that caters to all the patient's needs from check-in to discharge. The care-pair teams are cross-trained in functions ranging from EKG monitoring to housekeeping chores to recording patients' costs. Moreover, Lakeland has equipped patient rooms with computer terminals and mini-pharmacies so that the care pair has ready access to most necessities for providing quick, dependable service. Per-bed annual operating costs at the pilot unit are more than 9 percent lower than at conventionally organized units. Apart from this productivity boost, Lakeland's pilot unit is also enjoying higher patient satisfaction levels.[19] As this book goes to press, Lakeland Regional is expanding its successful pilot program to other units. According to Dr.

David T. Jones, Senior Vice President of Patient-Focused Development, the hospital hopes to implement the care-pair concept in all surgical units by the end of 1991.

Metropolitan Life Insurance Company is another company that extensively and profitably uses cross-functional teams to serve its group-insurance clients. John Falzon, Senior Vice President—Quality and Planning at MetLife, emphasizes the crucial role of customer-focused teamwork in delivering reliable service: "MetLife's Group Insurance products and service cannot be treated as 'off the shelf' items. We must respond to the specific needs and expectations of our customers and can do this only if we work together as participating team members. By viewing ourselves from the customer's perspective and involving all contributing functional units from the beginning, we prevent problems from happening."

Exhibit 2–4 describes a team-based approach developed by MetLife for designing and delivering defect-free services. This approach, in addition to emphasizing teamwork, underscores the importance of rigorously testing new services to ensure their reliability.

According to John Falzon, Senior Vice President – Quality and Planning at MetLife, based on experiences with a number of new-service introductions and the problems encountered therein, "MetLife has developed a process for preventing problems that starts at the very beginning when the decision is made to draft a proposal for new business or introduce a service." Mr. Falzon summarizes the steps involved in the process as follows:

- Formation of cross-functional teams. The team includes representatives from Administration, Claims, Marketing, and Information Systems. Together, they review all aspects of the proposed contract.

- Examination of key issues such as plan design, claim payment policies, utilization review controls, medical community relations, pricing, customer education, and systems.

- Team review of a draft proposal created by marketing and underwriting specialists. All areas provide input and work together to make certain that proposals meet customer expectations and that all promises and guarantees can be met.

- Development of claim volume estimates by the team. These projected figures form the basis for future staffing levels, including claim approvers and customer service personnel.

- Establishment of an 800 telephone number to handle questions that the prospective customer's employees may have prior to the date MetLife would start paying their claims.

Exhibit 2–4 MetLife's Process for Developing and Delivering Services

SUMMARY AND ACTION CHECKLIST

Service reliability—the extent to which the promised performance is delivered dependably and accurately—is the predominant criterion customers use in judging service quality which, in turn, is an essential springboard for launching marketing efforts that excel. Grand strategies for marketing a service, regardless of how clever, creative, and comprehensive they are, cannot be effective when customers perceive the service as unreliable.

The potential contributions of reliable service to marketing effectiveness include better customer retention, more business from existing customers, favorable word-of-mouth communications, and pricing premiums. Improving service reliability can also increase operating efficiency by lowering the cost of "rework," reducing service "scrap," boosting employee morale, and lowering employee turnover.

The pursuit of zero defects in services is in some ways more challenging than in manufacturing. The urgency associated with the need for performing and delivering error-free service in "real time," the subjectivity and "softness" of the criteria customers may use in evaluating service reliability, and the subtle ways in which a confusing service can increase service "scrap"—"avoidable customer input" in American Express terminology—complicate the task of assessing and improving service reliability.

Strong-willed leadership is essential for building and nurturing a company-wide culture wherein service reliability is paramount. Executives who persistently pursue perfection and frequently exhort employees to do likewise are crucial catalysts for continuously improving service reliability.

Rigorous pre-launch testing of new services and systematic post-launch monitoring to quickly rectify previously unanticipated service shortfalls are also essential for improving service reliability. Blueprinting services, conducting mystery shopper studies, and soliciting employee suggestions are some useful approaches for thoroughly testing services.

An infrastructure for error-free service is another supportive pillar for service reliability. This pillar rests on the foundation of employees who are willing, able, and encouraged to perform the service in exemplary fashion; effective teamwork among employees; and good communication systems.

We propose the following action checklist for management to improve service reliability:

1. *Do we believe that 100 percent reliability—zero service errors—is a worthwhile goal?* Are we convinced that improving reliability simultaneously can improve marketing effectiveness and operating efficiency? If not, what is the basis for our lack of conviction? Are we spending too much money on marketing and correcting an unreliable service when our resources could be better directed at performing the service right the first time?

2. *Do we have a good grasp of the challenges involved in striving for 100 percent service reliability?* Do we appreciate the fact that error-free service has to be delivered in real time? Do we know how much service "scrap" our operations generate as a result of poorly designed and communicated services?

3. *Do we demonstrate our commitment to service reliability to all our employees?* How often do executives talk to employees about the importance of striving for zero service errors? Is service reliability reiterated in all company communications? Is our quest for zero service errors prominently stated in our mission statement?

4. *Do we rigorously test new services prior to introduction?* Do we blueprint and fully understand the anatomy of every new service we develop? Do our customers and employees play active roles in designing the service? Do we "rehearse" the service with customers and employees?

5. *Do we continuously reevaluate our services after introduction?* Do we solicit, reward, and use feedback from employees to improve the service after it is introduced? Do we have a system in place for systematically capturing and analyzing customer complaints and concerns about the service?

6. *Are we doing enough to ensure that our employees are able, motivated, and encouraged to aim for zero service errors?* In hiring personnel, do we make a concerted effort to ensure that they are competent and committed to service excellence? Do we implement employee training programs that focus on how to provide flawless service? Do we sponsor formal, visible employee-recognition programs to celebrate the achievements of error-free service?

7. *Do we encourage, facilitate, and require teamwork and communication across functional units?* Do we have customer-focused interfunctional teams that are charged with ensuring reliable service? Can we foster interfunctional cohesion by implementing formal communication systems? Do we have programs to cross-train employees and to help them appreciate one another's jobs?

3

◇◇◇

Doing the Service Very
Right the Second Time

Relentless pursuit of flawless service is a hallmark of service excellence. Yet even exemplary companies that wholeheartedly embrace the philosophy of error-free service cannot escape service snafus altogether. Professors Christopher Hart, James Heskett, and Earl Sasser state this problem succinctly: "Mistakes are a critical part of every service. Hard as they try, even the best service companies can't prevent the occasional late flight, burned steak or missed delivery. The fact is, in services, often performed in the customer's presence, errors are inevitable."[1]

Does the inevitability of service errors mean a zero-service-defects goal is unworthy? Certainly not. As we argued in Chapter 2, the benefits of continuously improving service reliability—and the costs of failing to do so—are significant. What the inevitability of service shortfalls does imply is that excellent service recovery is just as critical as the pursuit of error-free service in building a quality-based foundation for marketing services. In this chapter, we discuss the rationale and present guidelines for engaging in an outstanding recovery effort when a service is flawed the first time.

RATIONALE FOR EXCELLENT SERVICE RECOVERY

Despite the current rhetoric in corporate circles about the importance of customer service, companies by and large do a poor job of righting the service wrongs their customers experience and endure. All too often, companies' responses—or lack thereof—leave complaining customers feeling worse instead of better. The high incidence of unsatisfactory response to service problems, which we demonstrate in the next section, is by itself reason enough for companies to strengthen their service recovery efforts. In addition, excellent service recovery provides a significant opportunity to reinforce relationships with customers and build customer loyalty.

SERVICE RECOVERY: A REPORT CARD

Escalating competition and more demanding customers have prodded many companies—in both goods and service sectors—to pay greater attention to *serving* their customers rather than merely *selling* to them. Has this increased emphasis on customer service improved the quality and effectiveness of companies' service recovery efforts? A comparison of two empirical studies separated by 13 years answers this question.

The first study was conducted by Professors Alan Andreasen and Arthur Best in 1975.[2] The second study was conducted by us and our colleague, Professor Valarie Zeithaml, in 1988.[3] Exhibit 3–1 briefly describes the two studies and summarizes relevant findings.

While the two studies had different objectives and used different sampling approaches, both examined survey respondents' perceived satisfaction with problem resolution. Moreover, both studies investigated multiple services. The data in Exhibit 3–1, therefore, offer an interesting then-versus-now comparison of service-recovery effectiveness.

Initially, the pattern of percentages in the last column of Exhibit 3–1 suggests an impressive improvement in service-recovery effectiveness during the period between the two studies. While the rate of satisfactory service problem resolution was only about one third to one half in 1975, it was about one half to two thirds in 1988. This optimistic interpretation, however, must be tempered by the fact that the 1988 study investigated the performance of five companies that were among the largest and most marketing-oriented in their industries. The rates of satisfactory problem resolution for services in general probably were lower than for the five companies investigated in the 1988 study. Moreover, the flip side of the 50 to 67 percent rate of effective service recovery is the 33 to 50 percent *ineffective* recovery. That even leading companies are failing to resolve satisfactorily a third or more of their customers' service problems is a striking finding that does not speak well of the current status of service-recovery

Exhibit 3–1 Incidence of Effective Service Recovery: 1975 vs. 1988

Authors and Year of Study	Nature of Study and Sample	Type of Service	Sample Size**	Percent of Sample Indicating Satisfactory Problem Resolution
Andreasen and Best—1975*	Customer-satisfaction study of a random sample of households in major metro areas in the United States; customer-satisfaction data on a variety of general product and service categories were collected	Home repair	78	53%
		Car repair	261	50%
		Credit	69	50%
		Film developing	84	45%
		Appliance repair	107	36%
		Medical/Dental care	84	35%
		Car parking	47	30%
Berry, Parasuraman, and Zeithaml —1988	Service-quality study of random samples of customers of five nationally known companies; data on customer assessment of various facets of each company's services were collected	Telephone repair (Co. 1)	148	67%
		Insurance (Co. 2)	137	66%
		Insurance (Co. 3)	73	59%
		Banking (Co. 4)	122	50%
		Banking (Co. 5)	119	56%

*The service-category labels and numbers in this part of the exhibit are from Exhibit IV in Alan R. Andreasen and Arthur Best, "Consumers Complain—Does Business Respond?" *Harvard Business Review,* July–August 1977, pp. 93–101.

**Number of respondents who experienced a problem in each category.

efforts. Clearly, while some progress may have been made, there is much room for improvement in handling and resolving service problems.

Apart from the findings in Exhibit 3–1, there are other indications that present service-recovery efforts are inadequate. Professors Andreasen and Best, in summarizing the conclusions from their 1975 customer-satisfaction study, assessed the prevailing company attitude toward resolving customer problems as quite negative: "Complaining consumers are often looked on by business as being 'the enemy.' . . . Those who deal with complaints may technically take care of the particular problem but still leave the customer angry: the 'enemy' mentality begins with the assumption that the customer is wrong."[4]

Has this propensity to perceive complaining customers as adversaries declined in the last 15 years? Not by much, according to recent comments made by John Goodman, President of Technical Assistance Research Programs (TARP), a leading customer-service research firm that has studied customer complaints and their consequences in a variety of industries. Admonishing service companies to shed their antagonistic posture, Goodman states: "Our research has found premeditated rip-offs [by complaining customers] represent 1 to 2 percent of the customer base in most organizations. However, most organizations defend themselves against unscrupulous customers by . . . treating the 98 percent of honest customers like crooks to catch the 2 percent who *are* crooks."[5]

In our own service-quality research, we have heard firsthand many frustrated customers bemoan the hostile, hurdle-ridden, and seemingly hopeless process that often awaits those who request rectification of defective services. Comments by participants in our focus groups illustrate:

A BANKING CUSTOMER: If you have a problem, they treat you like you have a disease.

A CREDIT CARD CUSTOMER: You can't get in touch with these people.

AN APPLIANCE REPAIR CUSTOMER: When you call in irate, who do you talk to? The office clerk who can't do anything.

The potential of ineffective recovery processes to aggravate unhappy customers further has been confirmed by other research as well. For instance, Professor Hart and his colleagues state: "Studies we've done show that more than half of all efforts to respond to customer complaints actually *reinforce* negative reactions to a service."[6]

The report card on the service sector's overall recovery effort looks mediocre. To be sure, exemplary companies renowned for their recovery efforts do exist. American Express, Federal Express, and L. L. Bean are examples. But these rare exceptions are far outnumbered by companies with no systems, or flawed systems, for service recovery.

BENEFITS OF STRONG SERVICE RECOVERY

Service-recovery situations have substantial potential for making a significant impression on customer perceptions of a company. Customers pay more attention to a company's performance when something goes awry than when everything goes smoothly. Flawed services—a hotel that has no room for a guest holding a guaranteed reservation, a waiter who spills soup on a customer, a credit-card statement showing charges for purchases a customer did not make—engender more intense customer emotion and evaluation than error-free services.

Drawing upon insights from the social-psychological literature, several researchers have suggested that customers react to routine services—those performed as planned—in a state of "mindlessness," characterized by minimal conscious attention and cognitive activity.[7] In contrast, customers encountering a nonroutine service situation snap out of their mindlessness and scrutinize the service company's handling of the situation. They are an attentive audience for the messages the company's recovery effort convey about its service values and priorities. Thus service-recovery situations offer some of the best opportunities for communicating commitment to customers and strengthening their loyalty.

Exhibit 3–2 illustrates the critical role service recovery plays in customers' assessment of a service. Based on research conducted by The First National Bank of Chicago, this exhibit lists the top ten of 25 attributes customers consider in evaluating bank services. Six of the ten attributes (shown in bold face) pertain directly to problem resolution and the four remaining attributes are indirectly relevant. Although developed in the context of bank services, the ten attributes are applicable to services in general. Clearly, a company's handling of service problems figures prominently in customers' perceptions of its service.

Our empirical research with customers of five large service companies confirms the critical influence of recovery efforts. As the findings summarized in Exhibit 3–3 consistently show, satisfactory problem resolution sharply increases customers' willingness to recommend the company and significantly improves their perceptions of the company's service quality.

Studies by other researchers have documented the monetary benefits of strong recovery efforts. For instance, according to TARP research, the average return from investments in problem-handling systems ranges from 100 percent (for marketers of durable goods such as washing machines and refrigerators) to 170 percent (for banks).[8]

The benefits of a strong recovery effort may not be uniformly high in all situations. As we argue in the next section, a company's reputation for being reliable—its record of performing the service right the

Exhibit 3–2 Top Ten Service Attributes of Importance to Customers

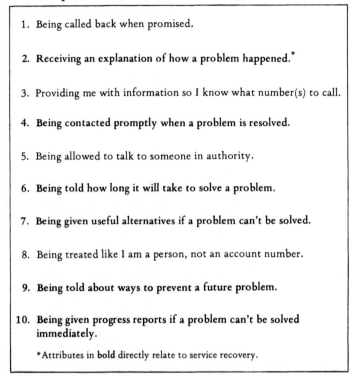

1. Being called back when promised.

2. Receiving an explanation of how a problem happened.*

3. Providing me with information so I know what number(s) to call.

4. **Being contacted promptly when a problem is resolved.**

5. Being allowed to talk to someone in authority.

6. **Being told how long it will take to solve a problem.**

7. **Being given useful alternatives if a problem can't be solved.**

8. Being treated like I am a person, not an account number.

9. **Being told about ways to prevent a future problem.**

10. **Being given progress reports if a problem can't be solved immediately.**

*Attributes in **bold** directly relate to service recovery.

SOURCE: Adapted from Linda Cooper and Beth Summer, *Getting Started in Quality,* Consumer Affairs/Quality Department, The First National Bank of Chicago, 1990, p. 27.

first time—is likely to influence the effectiveness of its recovery service.

THE SERVICE RELIABILITY-RECOVERY LINK

When a service problem occurs, a customer's confidence in the company may be shaken but won't be shattered except under two conditions:

1. The problem reinforces a recurring pattern of previous shortcomings.
2. The recovery effort fails to satisfy the customer, compounding rather than correcting the failure.

Exhibit 3–3 Impact of Strong vs. Weak Service Recovery

Company	Type of Service	Percent of Customers Willing to Recommend Company When Service Problems Were:		Customers' Overall Assessment of a Company's Service Quality When Service Problems Were:**	
		Not Resolved Satisfactorily*	Resolved Satisfactorily	Not Resolved Satisfactorily	Resolved Satisfactorily
1	Telephone Repair	13%	86%	−1.99	−0.74
2	Insurance	24%	82%	−2.24	−1.36
3	Insurance	31%	85%	−2.26	−1.06
4	Banking	21%	78%	−2.25	−1.33
5	Banking	54%	78%	−1.84	−0.90

*The 13% in the first row has the following interpretation: Of the Company 1 customers who perceived that their service problems were not resolved satisfactorily, 13% were willing to recommend the company to a friend. Other percentages have similar interpretations.

**Service quality scores measure customers' perceptions of the company relative to their expectations. If perceptions fall short of expectations, the company receives a minus score. The bigger the minus score, the worse the company's service quality.

The first condition implies serious problems with service reliability. As we discussed in Chapter 2, reliability is foremost to customers and forms the essential core of services marketing excellence. Little else matters to customers when a company's service is plagued by perennial problems. Excellent service recovery is not an effective cure for chronic unreliability. A car dealership that frequently fails to perform repairs right the first time, or an airline that often cancels flights at the last minute, cannot hope to regain customers' confidence merely through strong recovery efforts.

When a service problem is followed by a weak recovery effort— the second condition stated above—the company fails its customers twice, creating what Professor Mary Jo Bitner and her colleagues call a "double deviation" from customer expectations.[9] A double deviation will dramatically deflate customers' confidence in a company; when preceded by a history of unreliability, it will *devastate* customers' confidence and drive them to the competition.

Exhibit 3–4 portrays the likely impact of weak versus strong recovery efforts on customers' confidence in a company. The company's past record of providing reliable service has a bearing on how its recovery efforts influence customer confidence. When the com-

Exhibit 3–4 Differential Impact of Weak and Strong Recovery Efforts Under Different Reliability Levels

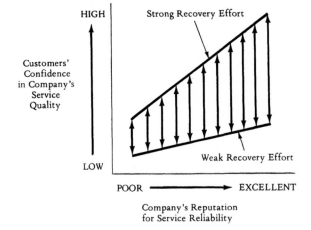

pany's reputation for service reliability is already poor, a weak recovery effort shatters whatever level of confidence might still exist. A strong recovery effort under these circumstances, while more effective than a weak recovery effort, is unlikely to provide a significant boost to customer confidence. As mentioned earlier, a strong recovery effort is not an effective cure for chronic unreliability. The marginal benefits of a strong over a weak recovery effort—represented by the double-headed, vertical arrows in Exhibit 3–4—increase as the reputation for service reliability improves. A strong recovery effort will have maximum impact when the company has a solid reputation for service reliability. In other words, excellent service reliability and an all-out recovery effort when occasional but inevitable service snafus do occur are the hallmarks of exemplary service companies.

GUIDELINES FOR EXCELLENT SERVICE RECOVERY

Excellent recovery is in some ways more difficult to achieve—and more tempting to downplay—than excellent reliability. Recovery situations are disruptions to the routine service process and often involve dealing with disgruntled customers. Not surprisingly, companies frequently respond to service problems grudgingly, if at all. The temptation to perceive problem situations as unproductive, unprofitable, and unpleasant interruptions can be quite strong, relegating service recovery to low-priority status.

Ironically, companies renowned for their service reliability are especially vulnerable to this temptation. Their record of performing the service right the first time much of the time may breed complacency and leave them ill-prepared and reluctant to deal effectively with occasional problems. Yet customer goodwill earned through several reliably performed service transactions can be badly damaged by just one poorly handled service problem.

Companies can ill afford to handle service problems in a half-hearted, haphazard fashion. To excel in and reap maximum benefits from problem resolution, companies must have in place a systematic, ongoing recovery process. While the specifics will vary from company to company, the recovery process should include the general components shown in Exhibit 3–5. The process has three principal stages (enclosed by the thick-lined boxes in Exhibit 3–5), which we now discuss.

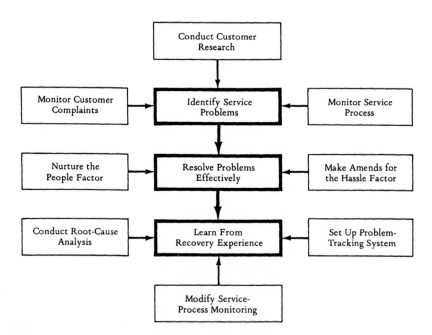

Exhibit 3–5 Essentials of Effective Service Recovery

IDENTIFY SERVICE PROBLEMS

Striving to unearth all customer disappointments—no matter how minor—is an essential first step in building a reputation for recovery excellence. Successfully exposing problems requires casting a wide net to capture customer grievances. To minimize the chances of service problems slipping through unnoticed, companies must have an effective system for monitoring customer complaints, conducting customer research, and monitoring the service process.

Monitor Customer Complaints. Examining comments volunteered by customers is one approach for identifying service deficiencies. Many companies currently use this approach, as evidenced by the pervasiveness of communication channels such as toll-free telephone lines, comment cards, and suggestion boxes available to customers. Even in the absence of these channels, customers can—and some invariably do—provide unsolicited feedback. Every company can benefit from an ongoing system for capturing and analyzing customer complaints.

To be effective, an ongoing complaint-handling system must initiate prompt internal action to resolve the complaints it receives. It also must trigger prompt external action to apologize to complaining customers, to acknowledge the company's awareness of their dissatisfaction, and to inform them of the corrective measures being taken. However, systems for reacting to customer complaints, regardless of their effectiveness and responsiveness, are insufficient for service-recovery excellence. Extensive research has documented that many customers who experience problems simply choose not to complain because they perceive no efficient, hassle-free way to complain or believe complaining will not make any difference.[10]

The availability of conduits such as toll-free telephone lines will not encourage disgruntled customers to complain if they believe that companies really do not care—a belief frequently reinforced by constantly busy phones or by unhelpful, unsympathetic responses when customers finally reach a company representative. Moreover, only customers experiencing serious problems are likely to complain on their own. In fact, research conducted by TARP has shown that 31 percent of customers facing an average potential loss of $142 due to defective products or services still did not complain.[11]

A company cannot achieve service-recovery excellence if it relies exclusively on volunteered complaints to identify trouble spots. One way to become aware of complaints that customers do not bother to lodge is to ferret them out through research.

Conduct Customer Research. Soliciting complaints through formal or informal research is a necessary supplement to monitoring volunteered complaints. Taking the initiative to solicit complaints demonstrates a level of caring and concern that waiting for customers to volunteer complaints lacks. Dissatisfied customers who are normally too skeptical to bother to call a toll-free number or complete a comment card will be more inclined to air their grievances if they sense genuine company interest.

Customer research aimed at identifying service problems can be qualitative or quantitative and can be approached through questioning as well as observation. Embassy Suites Hotel conducts 350 open-ended interviews with guests every day, supplemented by a structured survey of 6,000 guests every year. The Cadillac Division of General Motors, a recent winner of the Malcolm Baldrige National Quality Award, regularly conducts customer focus groups in 25 "listening post" dealerships to identify problems. It also analyzes every repair order and complaint received by these dealerships.[12]

The Marriott Corporation, in addition to providing guests with an easily accessible 24-hour "hot line," has trained its employees to be proactive in identifying—and solving—service problems by playing the role of observer-researchers. A business customer at one Marriott hotel who wanted to hold a meeting with several associates in the concierge lounge was worrying aloud about the lack of privacy there. An observant hotel employee who overheard this customer's concern immediately contacted the front desk and located a vacant suite where the guest and his associates could meet in private.[13] As this anecdote demonstrates, service employees should be trained and encouraged to be attentive observers, ready to recognize problems as they occur. Roger Dow, Vice President of Sales and Marketing at Marriott, makes this point well: "The guest-contact employee is the only one close enough to the customer to recognize and evaluate a problem and make it right for the customer and keep that customer. These points are brought up over and over again in the training of our employees." Alert employees can spot service shortfalls—and opportunities to pleasantly surprise customers—that otherwise might escape a company's attention.

Another observation approach for identifying service deficiencies is to employ mystery shoppers—researchers posing as customers—to experience and evaluate the service. Virtually every type of service—from air travel to auto repair, from entertainment to equipment rental, from hospitality to health care—is amenable to observation by mystery shoppers.

Monitor Service Process. Observing the service through the eyes of employees or mystery shoppers is one form of service monitoring. The problems identified through such transaction-specific monitoring, however, are invariably visible to and being experienced by customers. While it is important to recognize and resolve these problems, a strong, proactive recovery process must attempt to anticipate problems before customers experience them. Identifying potential trouble spots will give a company a head start in its recovery efforts—by minimizing the need for recovery through problem prevention, and by allowing additional time for preparing (e.g., summoning extra service representatives) to handle effectively the problems that do crop up.

Anticipating service problems requires internal, behind-the-scenes monitoring of the general service process. One approach for internal monitoring is to scrutinize a service blueprint—a type of flow chart that exposes the anatomy of the service—to identify fail points where the service is subject to potential breakdowns.[14] Jane Kingman-Brundage, a consultant specializing in service-system design, uses a variation of service blueprints, called *service maps,* to portray the relationships among customers, front-line employees, and support employees. In her words: "Service maps [depict] the chronology of tasks involved in rendering the service [and] highlight crucial points where the consumer is 'handed-off' from one work group to another." Because instances where customers are transferred from one service employee or function to another are vulnerable to glitches, service maps are especially helpful in uncovering fail points.

Another approach that can be used in conjunction with service blueprints and maps is to track and analyze past failures systematically, a topic we will discuss later in the chapter. Once potential fail points are identified, they must be watched carefully and constantly for signs of trouble, and contingency plans must be devised for dealing effectively with breakdowns when they occur.

Of course, not all service problems can be identified before customers experience them. But many can be, through systematic monitoring of the service process to detect problems in the making. Consider patients who arrive at their doctor's office on time only to be told that the doctor is running an hour late; or appliance-repair customers kept waiting for hours beyond the time the repair person was scheduled to show up; or airline customers who, upon arrival at the airport, are informed that their flight was canceled hours earlier. In these and similar instances, frustrated customers frequently are left to suffer in silence. Customers summoning enough willpower to complain often are confronted by harried and abrupt service personnel who are ill-prepared to deal with the breakdown. Yet, in situations like these the company could anticipate customer frustration and take steps to alleviate it, including calling customers to warn them of the problem and apologizing in advance.

Failing to devise and implement a proactive recovery effort is often a more serious shortfall in customers' eyes than the basic problem which, in a genuine emergency, customers are likely to recognize and excuse as being unavoidable. Anticipatory monitoring of the service process will help minimize such failures and provide a significant competitive advantage in markets where proactive recovery efforts are rare.

RESOLVE PROBLEMS EFFECTIVELY

In Chapter 2, we introduced five quality dimensions as principal criteria customers use in evaluating a service: reliability, tangibles, responsiveness, assurance, and empathy. Of these, reliability primarily concerns the service *outcome,* while the others are more concerned with the service *process.*[15] A service failure is essentially a flawed *outcome* that reflects a breakdown in reliability—an erroneous bank statement, an improperly repaired automobile, luggage lost on an airline trip. Even though reliability is of foremost concern to customers during initial performance of a service, the process dimensions assume prominence during recovery service. John Farley, Total Quality Manager of Corning's Industrial Products Division (a division that regularly measures its customers' service-quality perceptions on the five dimensions), makes this point well:

> Reliability, or doing it right the first time, is by far the most important dimension of service as seen from numerous survey responses. This is quickly becoming just as much a condition of doing business as having a competitive product or price. What is remembered, however, is how you reacted when you didn't do it right the first time. The other service dimensions of empathy, assurance, responsiveness and tangibles then come to the forefront.

Nurture the People Factor. Excellent recovery requires excellence in the process dimensions of service. And this requires excellent people. Three of the four process dimensions—responsiveness, assurance, and empathy—result *directly* from human performance.[16] Even low-contact services that typically involve little interaction between customers and company personnel (e.g., automatic teller machines, cable television, long-distance telephone, mail orders) become high-contact services when problems arise. Therefore, regardless of the type of service, employees who staff problem-resolution positions by and large determine whether the recovery effort regenerates customer confidence or degenerates into a double deviation.

We offer the following suggestions for stimulating employee behavior that maximizes the likelihood of converting a problem situation into a positive one for both customer and company.

1. *Prepare Employees for Recovery.* Employee responses to service problems cannot be left to chance. While some employees may be naturally responsive, reassuring, and empathetic in dealing with customers experiencing problems, most are not. Even employees who exhibit exemplary behavior during routine transactions may come unglued in dealing with problem situations. Inability or unwillingness of service personnel to respond effectively to exceptions is a pervasive problem. An extensive study by Professor Bitner and her colleagues found that almost 43 percent of unsatisfactory service encounters were failure situations handled poorly by employees.[17]

Proper training to make service personnel equally effective in performing their routine and recovery roles is imperative. As Hart, Heskett, and Sasser state: "In addition to following rules, sticking to a routine, and treating every situation alike no matter what, front-line workers must be able to do the opposite: bend the rules, take initiative, and improvise. Building a staff that can do both requires rigorous and conscious effort and is at the heart of a company's ability to recover from service mishaps."[18]

Exhibit 3–6 describes key recovery skills that service-personnel training should foster. Properly training personnel before placing them in problem-resolution positions is a prudent investment. At Federal Express, the first service company to win the Malcolm Baldrige National Quality Award, customer service representatives receive five weeks of training before they are assigned to one of 15 service centers around the country. The representatives also receive four hours of recurrent training per month. They are prepared so

<u>Communication Skills.</u> Recovery situations invariably involve dealing with frustrated customers. Helping those customers vent their frustrations and defusing their anger are essential for effective problem resolution. As John Goodman, President of TARP, and his colleagues, state: "An angry customer is irrational and unwilling to negotiate reasonable solutions. Thus, the first step in resolving a fuming customer's problem is to deal with the customer's anger."[19] Encouraging customers to express their grievances, listening to them patiently and attentively, acknowledging and apologizing for their hardship, and making them feel like friends rather than foes are important traits that training should emphasize. General courses designed to improve interpersonal skills as well as service-specific role-playing exercises and videotapes depicting "how to" and "how not to" scenarios can be used to improve service employees' communication skills.

<u>Creativity.</u> Dealing effectively and expeditiously with exceptions requires resourcefulness on the part of service employees. Some would argue that creativity is a natural trait and cannot be taught. However, training sessions that use games, exercises, and other devices to sharpen service employees' problem-solving and improvisation skills will, at a minimum, sensitize employees to the need for being resourceful and stimulate whatever innate but dormant creative skills they possess. Periodic participation in such sessions will be particularly beneficial to employees accustomed to performing the same service in robot-like fashion. Sonesta Hotels and the American Association of Homes for the Aging are two organizations that use custom-designed, service-specific games in their training programs.[20]

<u>Competence.</u> Recipients of recovery service are giving a company a second chance to win back their confidence. The competence of service representatives and their ability to demonstrate it are crucial to reassuring customers and regaining their confidence. Several of the important recovery aspects highlighted in Exhibit 3-2 relate to employee competence — explaining how the problem happened, estimating when it will be solved, suggesting useful alternatives if it cannot be solved, offering tips on preventing its recurrence. Our focus-group research on service quality has revealed many instances wherein the competence conveyed by service representatives in recovery situations made the critical difference between customer satisfaction and dissatisfaction. The following comments from focus-group participants illustrate:

- The repairman not only fixed my broken washing machine but also explained to me what had gone wrong and how I might be able to fix it myself if a similar problem occurred in the future.

  —An elated home-appliance repair customer

- Sometimes you are quoting stuff from their instruction manuals to their own people and they don't even know what it means.

  —A disgruntled business-equipment repair customer

Giving service employees sufficient competence — and confidence — to handle recovery situations requires thorough training on the technical aspects of the services they perform and appropriate cross-training to help them see how what they do relates to what others in the organization do. Periodic retraining is necessary to update employees' knowledge and skills as the nature of the services or the means of delivering them change.

<u>Understanding Customers' Benefit Expectations.</u> Not all customers experiencing similar problems expect the same benefits from the recovery effort. Findings from several studies have documented this variation in benefit expectations.[21] A customer's assessment of a recovery effort depends on the extent to which it meets what the customer hoped to get from it. Service representatives who are able to gauge customer expectations and tailor their recovery response accordingly will be more effective and efficient than those who provide a standard response. While an expression of apology and concern for the customer's trouble should be standard in every recovery effort — and might be all it takes to appease some customers — it would rarely be sufficient to satisfy all disgruntled customers. On the other hand, "giving away the store" to every dissatisfied customer would be wasteful and unnecessary because not all customers would expect it.

Determining what would make a disgruntled customer happy is largely a function of the service representative's communication skills — especially listening and probing skills as well as the ability to sense and interpret nonverbal cues that the customer's body language might convey. Therefore, a segment of the communication-skills training of service representatives should focus specifically on the importance of and guidelines for understanding the benefits each customer hopes to receive from the problem-resolution process.

Exhibit 3–6 Recovery Skills That Training Should Develop and Reinforce

well that they solve a large percentage of customer problems without having to refer them to higher levels, of which Federal Express has two in its recovery system: trace agents and an executive services group. Says John West, Manager of Quality Improvement: "The [recovery] system has become so efficient that nothing escapes the net. I may take care of three customer problems a week because everything has been headed off closer to the line. My phone would be ringing off the hook if our front-line people were not legitimately trained and empowered to handle customer needs."[22]

2. *Empower Employees.* Giving employees the authority to satisfy customers is as critical as training employees to be effective problem solvers. Training without empowerment is not conducive to a strong recovery effort. This is why Federal Express's customer service representatives are trained *and empowered* to resolve problems as John West states. Although the average Federal Express transaction costs only $16, the company's service representatives are empowered to spend up to $100 to resolve a customer problem.

Employees of Satisfaction Guaranteed Eateries, Inc., a highly successful Seattle restaurant chain whose motto is synonymous with its name, have wide authority to please customers. Timothy Firnstahl, CEO and founder of the restaurant chain, says: "I instituted the idea that employees could and should do *anything* to keep the customer happy. In the event of an error or delay, any employee right down to the busboy could provide complementary wine or desserts, or pick up an entire tab if necessary."[23]

3. *Facilitate Employees.* Companies renowned for their recovery efforts supplement training and empowerment with technology and information to augment the ability of their customer service representatives to resolve problems effectively. Among several systems supporting Federal Express's service representatives is a state-of-the-art telephone system. This system instantly routes calls among the company's 15 service centers to the next available agent, permitting a response within two rings in most cases and an impressively low rate of abandoned calls (less than .005 percent of 290,000 calls received each day). The phone system also keeps track of customers whose calls are abandoned initially so that service representatives can recontact them, apologize, and offer to help.

American Express is another company with a huge investment in technology to support well-trained, empowered customer service representatives who solve *on the spot* 85 percent of the problems that prompt customers to call them. They key billing or other changes directly into an on-line data system, and these adjustments are reflected in the customer's next statement. American Express's reputation for problem-resolution service is unrivaled in the credit-card sector.[24]

Customer service representatives also need psychological support to perform at their peak. Providing routine service to customers with different demands and demeanors day after day is itself hard, stressful work. Providing *recovery* service is even harder and more stressful as the recipients of this service typically are disgruntled customers with a less than congenial disposition. Companies should make a concerted effort to explore ways for assisting their service-recovery staff to relieve tension. Courses on coping with stress, group meetings with peers to discuss job-related pressures, and facilities for physical exercise are some of the possibilities. Providing customer service personnel with a pleasant and soothing work environment also will be helpful. Telephone representatives at Digital Equipment Corporation's customer support center in Colorado Springs sit next to glass windows through which they can peer at Pike's Peak. (Managers at the center have windowless offices.)[25]

4. *Reward Employees.* Training, empowering, and providing support systems for recovery-service personnel will prepare but not necessarily persuade them to excel in problem resolution. Appropriate rewards are essential to fully unleash employee potential for providing exemplary recovery service. Rewarding excellent recovery efforts also serves to demonstrate the genuineness of management's commitment and to dispel any skepticism on the part of newly empowered employees.

When employees of Satisfaction Guaranteed Eateries were first given free rein to please dissatisfied customers, they approached their authority with a healthy dose of hesitation. They found it hard to believe that management would not penalize them for giving away free food and drinks. Overcoming this skepticism required intense positive reinforcement, including generous cash awards for employees of restaurants with exceptionally good problem-resolution and complaint-reduction rates.[26]

To motivate all service representatives to be good at problem resolution and to encourage the good ones to become better, a reward system might:

- Offer several levels of awards with varying degrees of visibility and recognition to reflect different levels of recovery excellence

- Make available a relatively large number of awards at lower levels to place them within reach of anyone willing to put forth a sincere, all-out recovery effort
- Give fewer awards at higher levels and be more stringent in making those awards
- Publicize widely and prominently the specific accomplishments of higher-level awardees as shining examples of excellent recovery and as inspiration for peers

Make Amends for the Hassle Factor. A service problem is at best an inconvenience to a customer. At worst it can be a major burden. Regardless of the severity, however, the customer incurs some monetary cost (e.g., expense of returning to seek redress) or nonmonetary cost (e.g., frustration, lost time), or both, *even if the problem is ultimately resolved.* In other words, whenever customers experience a service problem, they are forced to sacrifice something they would not have to if the service had been performed right the first time. Firnstahl refers to this sacrifice as the "hassle factor."[27]

An excellent service recovery effort must make amends for the hassle factor. Companies must do more for the customer than merely reperforming the service. Following the suggestions we made earlier in this chapter—e.g., making it easy for customers to complain; being proactive in spotting and correcting problems; empowering employees to make speedy, on-the-spot reparations—will go a long way in mitigating the hassle factor. But mere mitigation will not completely compensate a customer. A truly exceptional problem-resolution process will make customers feel they gained more than they gave up in going through the recovery experience.

When Minneapolis's First Bank System mishandled a direct payroll deposit for a client company, it sent every employee of the company a $15 check and an apology. It also gave employees the name and telephone number of a bank representative who could answer questions and resolve problems.[28]

Three months after Toyota's hot-selling Lexus automobile was introduced in the United States, the company received complaints from two owners (out of 8,000 who had purchased the car at that point). One complaint was about a defective brake light and the other concerned a sticky cruise-control mechanism. Toyota immediately recalled *all* 8,000 cars for replacement of the potentially defective parts. Impressively, the car owners were not subjected to the usual hassle of taking their cars to their dealerships. Instead, their cars were picked up, repaired, and returned to them. One Detroit dealer who had sold the model to ten owners in Grand Rapids, 150 miles from Detroit, flew in a crew of technicians to Grand Rapids, rented garage space, picked up the cars, repaired them, and washed them before returning them.[29] Some readers may argue that Toyota overreacted and went far beyond what was necessary. We would argue that Toyota capitalized on an opportunity to strengthen customers' confidence, exceed customers' expectations (Chapter 4), build customer relationships (Chapter 8), and stimulate favorable word-of-mouth advertising for a new automobile (Chapter 1). In short, we would argue that Toyota was practicing excellent services marketing.

LEARN FROM RECOVERY EXPERIENCE

Problem-resolution situations are more than just opportunities to fix flawed services and strengthen ties with customers. They are also a valuable—but frequently ignored or underutilized—source of diagnostic, prescriptive information for improving customer service. Corning's John Farley describes a problem-resolution situation as "a gift, an opportunity to learn how to get better." A company can and should learn as much as possible from each recovery experience. Effective learning involves searching for and correcting the underlying cause of the service shortfall, readjusting the monitoring of the service process, and implementing an information system to track problems.

Conduct Root-Cause Analysis. Service failures experienced by customers are typically symptoms of more serious problems in the service system. Doing everything necessary to appease customers and compensate them for the failures is, of course, an important part of a strong recovery effort. But it is seldom sufficient if preventing the recurrence of failures is a goal. To be fully beneficial, the recovery effort must strive to ferret out and fix the root causes of the failures.

Joseph Riesenman, Managing Director of Quality & Measurement Services at NYNEX Service Company, emphasizes the need for conducting root-cause analysis: "Learn from the breakdown. That is, don't go for a quick fix when a long-term solution is required. The quick fix or temporary expedient will probably break down again at some future time, cost a company more in the long term, and negatively impact the company's ability to compete effectively in the marketplace." Michael English, Director—Quality Positioning at GTE Telephone Operations, echoes Riesenman's advice: "Ensure root-cause analysis is conducted routinely to prevent recurring problems/ defects from affecting the customer."

Timothy Firnstahl firmly believes that employee failures in his restaurants are merely symptoms of system failures. And he insists that recovery efforts triggered by employee failures include an in-depth search to expose and correct underlying system failures. Firnstahl's insistence on conducting root-cause analysis has paid off repeatedly and handsomely as his narration of the following story illustrates.

> Our kitchens were turning out wrong orders at a rate that was costing us thousands of dollars a month in wasted food. The cooks insisted that the food servers were punching incorrect orders into the kitchen printout computer. In times past, we might have ended our search right there, accused the food servers of sloppiness, and asked everyone to be more careful. But now, adhering to the principle of system failure not people failure, we looked beyond the symptoms and found a flaw in our training. We had simply never taught food servers to double-check their orders on the computer screen, and the system offered no reward for doing so. Mistakes plummeted as soon as we started training people properly and handing out awards each month for the fewest ordering errors and posting lists of the worst offenders (no punishments, just names).[30]

Modify Service-Process Monitoring. Monitoring the service process is a strategy discussed earlier for proactive identification of service problems. Knowledge gained through systematically tracking and analyzing past failures may suggest changes in the monitoring process to make it more effective. For instance, a recurring pattern of patient complaints about unresponsive nurses in a hospital might suggest closer than usual scrutiny of patient-nurse encounters to identify possible areas for improvement. As this example implies, appropriately modifying how the service process is monitored and conducting root-cause analysis are interrelated: the former can assist in the search for underlying causes of recurring service problems. Performing root-cause analysis of an individual service problem, in turn, may reveal previously unrecognized fail points in the service process worthy of future monitoring.

Set Up Problem-Tracking System. An ongoing system that captures information pertaining to each instance of recovery service (e.g., information about the customer experiencing the problem, the nature of the problem, and the actions taken in response to the problem) is essential for maximizing the benefits from a company's service-recovery efforts. Methodically searching for underlying causes of service problems and identifying opportunities for improving service reliability will be difficult without a problem-tracking system. Such a system will serve as a solid foundation for capitalizing on the learning opportunity created by a company's recovery experiences.

The tracking system must be updated continuously to quickly spot potential trouble as well as new insights for improving service. To ensure the system stays current, customer service representatives should be able to key information directly into it. Direct access to the system will also facilitate retrieval of relevant information (e.g., past history of problems experienced by a complaining customer) helpful to the representatives in their recovery efforts. Finally, to make full use of the information in the system, management should receive, discuss, and act on regular reports summarizing the type and frequency of service problems.

Companies well-known for their recovery-service excellence, such as Federal Express and American Express, have sophisticated direct-access information systems. Companies that want to initiate a problem-tracking system or upgrade an existing one can now obtain advice and technical support from several specialized firms. Software systems for recording, tracking, and analyzing customer complaints are also available.[31]

SUMMARY AND ACTION CHECKLIST

Even companies with a reputation for service excellence experience service failures. However, not all is lost when service fails. A strong recovery effort can restore customer confidence and reinforce customer loyalty.

Yet many companies do not capitalize on the opportunity service recovery creates for strengthening customer ties. They respond to service problems and complaining customers reluctantly, if at all. Companies' recovery efforts still leave many customers dissatisfied, often reinforcing rather than reducing their negative feelings.

Customers are more emotionally involved in—and more attentive observers of—recovery service than routine service. How a company handles and resolves service problems, therefore, has a disproportionately significant impact on customers' perceptions of service quality. Service-recovery excellence coupled with a reputation for service reliability is a powerful, profitable strategy for gaining and retaining customers.

We offer the following action checklist for achieving service-recovery excellence:

1. *Do we have an effective system for capturing complaints volunteered by customers?* Do we encourage customers to voice their grievances? Do we make it easy for customers to complain (e.g., offer a toll-free number with sufficient telephone lines)?

2. *Do we conduct formal research on customers' service problems?* Do we include questions in surveys about customer service problems? Do we use qualitative research techniques (e.g., customer focus groups) to identify problems with our service? Are our employees trained to be attentive listeners and observers to spot service problems?

3. *Do we systematically monitor potential fail points in our service?* Is spotting potential problems before our customers do a priority in our company? What internal checks of our service process do we have in place? If we do not have any, why not?

4. *Are our employees prepared and encouraged to excel in resolving service problems?* Do we formally train our employees in service recovery? Are communication, creativity, and stress-management skills emphasized in our training programs in addition to relevant technical skills? Are our employees empowered to resolve customer problems with a minimum of red tape? Do we recognize and reward employees for providing excellent recovery service?

5. *Are we sensitive to the hassle factor customers experience in getting service problems resolved?* Have we taken steps to minimize customer hardship? To ensure fast response? Do we make it a point to do something extra for customers who experience problems with our service?

6. *Do we strive to expose the root causes of service problems?* Do we believe that most problems customers encounter are merely symptoms of more serious service-system failures? Do we formally assign an individual or a team to investigate the underlying causes of recurring problems?

7. *Do we modify our service-process monitoring based on recovery experiences?* Are we alert to previously unrecognized fail

points? Do we adjust our service monitoring as needed to facilitate and incorporate insights from root-cause analyses?

8. *Do we have an effective problem-tracking system?* If yes, is the information in the system analyzed regularly to uncover new insights for improving service quality? Is the system updated continuously? Do our customer service representatives have access to it?

4

◇◇◇

Managing and Exceeding Customers' Expectations

Customers' expectations play a pivotal role in judging a company's service. Customers assess service quality by comparing what they want or expect with what they perceive they are getting.[1] To earn a reputation for quality service, companies must consistently perform at levels customers perceive as meeting or surpassing their expectations. Customers are the sole judges of service quality. Management may think the company's service is fine, but if customers disagree the company has a problem.

That the discrepancy between expectations and perceptions is the primary determinant of customers' service-quality assessments is widely acknowledged in the literature.[2] However, the term *expectations* as a comparison standard is commonly used in two different ways—what customers believe *will occur* in a service encounter (predictions) and what customers *want to occur* (desires).[3] Moreover, there is no underlying conceptual framework for integrating different types of expectations and understanding their influence on customers' service-performance assessments.

With our colleague, Valarie Zeithaml, we devoted the latest phase of our ongoing service-quality research program to studying customers' service expectations. We conducted 16 customer focus group interviews in six service sectors to investigate the nature and sources of customers' service expectations and to explore how companies could meet and exceed them.[4] Our study covered automobile insurance, commercial property and casualty insurance, business equipment repair, truck and tractor rental/leasing, automobile repair, and hotels. Much of what we discuss in this chapter is based on consistent findings from this multi-sector study. We begin with a discussion of the basic structure of expectations.

STRUCTURE OF CUSTOMERS' EXPECTATIONS

TWO LEVELS OF EXPECTATIONS

Our findings indicate that customers' service expectations exist at two different levels: a *desired* level and an *adequate* level. The desired service level reflects the service the customer hopes to receive. It is a blend of what the customer believes "can be" and "should be." The adequate service level reflects what the customer finds acceptable. It is, in part, a function of the customer's assessment of what the service "will be," i.e., the customer's *predicted* service level.

A *zone of tolerance* separates the desired and adequate service levels as shown in Exhibit 4–1. The zone of tolerance is a range of service performance that a customer considers satisfactory. A performance level below the tolerance zone will engender customer frustration and decrease customer loyalty. A performance level above the tolerance zone will pleasantly surprise customers and strengthen their loyalty.

To illustrate, consider a bank customer who wishes to have a check cashed in three minutes (desired service level). However, based

```
┌─────────────────────────────┐
│       Desired Service        │
├─────────────────────────────┤
│░░░░░░░░░░░░░░░░░░░░░░░░░░░░░░░│
│░░░░░░░░░░░░░░░░░░░░░░░░░░░░░░░│
│░░░░░░░░░░░Zone░░░░░░░░░░░░░░░░│
│░░░░░░░░░░░of░░░░░░░░░░░░░░░░░░│
│░░░░░░░░Tolerance░░░░░░░░░░░░░░│
│░░░░░░░░░░░░░░░░░░░░░░░░░░░░░░░│
│░░░░░░░░░░░░░░░░░░░░░░░░░░░░░░░│
├─────────────────────────────┤
│      Adequate Service        │
└─────────────────────────────┘
```

Exhibit *4–1* Two Levels of Expectations

on past experience, number of customers waiting to be served, time of day, and other factors, the customer is willing to tolerate a total transaction time of ten minutes (adequate service level). Thus, if the total transaction time is within the range of three to ten minutes (zone of tolerance), the customer will be satisfied with the bank's speed of service. However, a total transaction time falling outside the zone of tolerance will make a much stronger impression (favorable if the time is less than three minutes and unfavorable if it is greater than ten minutes) on the customer's perception of speed of service.

The zone of tolerance can vary from customer to customer and, potentially, from transaction to transaction for the same customer. The zone of tolerance also differs across the five key dimensions customers use in evaluating a service: reliability, tangibles, responsiveness, assurance, and empathy.[5] In general, the greater a dimension's importance, the smaller is its zone of tolerance, reflecting less customer willingness to relax service standards.

Our previous research has shown repeatedly that customers value reliability—keeping the service promise—above all other dimensions. Moreover, as discussed in Chapter 3, reliability largely concerns the service outcome, i.e., *whether* the promised service is delivered. The remaining four dimensions relate more to the service process, i.e., *how* the service is delivered. Our expectations study confirmed that customers view reliability as the service "core" and are least tolerant of broken service promises. Therefore, the zone of tolerance for the outcome dimension of reliability is likely to be narrower, and the boundaries defining the zone (i.e., the desired and adequate service levels) are likely to be higher. Exhibit 4–2 portrays our hypothesized difference between the tolerance zones for the service outcome and process dimensions.

CHANGES IN EXPECTATION LEVELS

Our focus groups provided considerable evidence that customers' expectation levels are dynamic and fluctuate in response to a variety of factors. While both levels fluctuate, the desired service level tends to change more slowly and in smaller amounts than the adequate service level. The desired service level is also more likely to rise, whereas the adequate service level appears to move readily up or down. Thus, the variation in the zone of tolerance is akin to an accordion's movement, with most of the variation resulting from fluc-

Exhibit 4–2 Zones of Tolerance for Outcome and Process Dimensions of Service

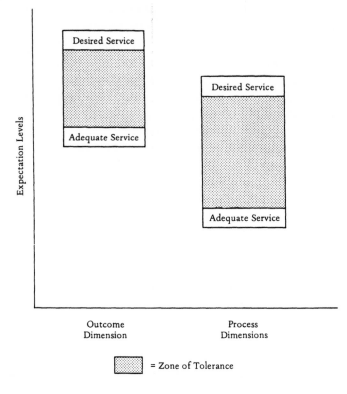

= Zone of Tolerance

tuations in the adequate service level rather than the desired service level.

Factors that could influence customers' expectation levels and induce changes in their tolerance zones include *enduring service intensifiers, personal needs, transitory service intensifiers, perceived service alternatives, self-perceived service role, explicit service promises, implicit service promises, word-of-mouth communications,* and *past experience*. Exhibit 4–3 defines these factors and illustrates each with comments made by focus group participants.

The nature of these factors and the basic bi-level structure of service expectations suggest several strategies for effectively managing and exceeding expectations (summarized in Exhibit 4–4). Managing expectations, as Exhibit 4–4 shows, lays the foundation for and contributes to exceeding expectations which, in turn, is the basis for

Exhibit 4-3 Factors Influencing Expectation Levels and Zones of Tolerance

Factors and Definitions	Illustrative Focus Group Comments
Enduring Service Intensifiers: Factors that intensify the customer's sensitivity to service on an ongoing basis (e.g., expectations of an affiliated party such as the customer's customer)	* Business equipment repair customer: "Expectations come from the customers I serve; for example, the doctors who use our blood tests. They have high expectations and therefore I have high expectations." * Truck leasing customer: "My expectations are higher today because of changes in the business world. It is a just-in-time inventory world today. People are impatient."
Personal Needs: Individual requirements dictated by customer-specific physical, psychological, social, or resource characteristics	* Business insurance customer: "I expect the broker to do a great deal of my work because I don't have the staff .... I expect the broker to know a great deal about my business and communicate that knowledge to the underwriter." * Another business insurance customer (with lower expectations): "My expectations are different ..... I do have a staff to do our certificates, etc., and use the broker minimally."
Transitory Service Intensifiers: Factors that heighten the customer's sensitivity to service on a temporary basis (e.g., personal emergencies, problems with the initial service)	* Automobile insurance customer: "The nature of my problem influences my expectations; for example, a broken window versus a DWI accident requiring brain surgery." * Automobile repair customer: "I am willing to be understanding the first time but would expect much more and be more impatient the second time around."
Perceived Service Alternatives: Customers' perceptions of the degree to which they have options in obtaining the service	* Hotel customer: "When your options are limited, you take the best you can get. My expectations are not necessarily lower but my tolerance level is higher." * Business insurance customer: "Sometimes you just don't have many options so you have to effectively settle for less."

Exhibit 4–3 Continued

Factors and Definitions	Illustrative Focus Group Comments
<u>Self-Perceived Service Role</u>: Customers' perceptions of the degree to which they themselves influence the level of service they receive	* Automobile insurance customer: "You can't blame it all on the insurance agent. You need to be responsible, too, and let the agent know what exactly you want." * Truck leasing customer: "There are a lot of variables that can influence how you get treated, including how you deal with them."
<u>Explicit Service Promises</u>: Company statements about the service made to customers (e.g., advertising, personal selling, contracts)	* Hotel customer: "They get you real pumped up with the beautiful ad. When you go in, you expect the bells and whistles to go off. Usually they don't." * Business insurance customer: "We leave them for obvious, common sense reasons. They don't honor the claim."
<u>Implicit Service Promises</u>: Service-related cues other than explicit promises that lead to inferences about what the service should or will be like (e.g., price, tangibles associated with the service)	* Business equipment repair customer: "If you are paying big bucks for these pieces of equipment, you expect more in the way of service." * Hotel customer: "You expect the service to be better in a nice-looking hotel."
<u>Word-of-Mouth Communications</u>: Statements made by parties other than the company about what the service will be like. These statements may come from both personal (e.g., friends) and "expert" (e.g., Consumer Reports) sources	* Hotel customer: "Personal reference, word-of-mouth, is always the best form of advertising." * Business insurance customer: "What you hear from others about higher service levels offered by their companies influences my expectation levels . . . . I will check around to see why my company isn't providing the same level of service."
<u>Past Experience</u>: Customers' previous exposure to service that is relevant to the present service	* Truck leasing customer: "I have gone from pricing to good service. I no longer go automatically with the low bidder." * Hotel customer: "As I've grown and learned more, I now have more to compare with."

Exhibit 4–4 Establishing a Customer Franchise Through Managing and Exceeding Expectations

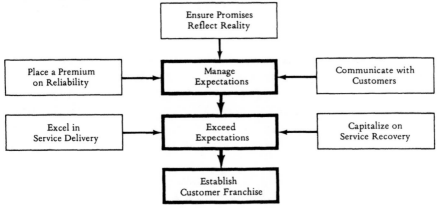

establishing a customer franchise (i.e., earning intense customer loyalty).

MANAGING CUSTOMERS' EXPECTATIONS

Companies can manage expectations effectively by managing the service promises they make, by dependably performing the promised service, and by effectively communicating with customers.

ENSURE PROMISES REFLECT REALITY

Of the various potential determinants of expectations defined in Exhibit 4–3, explicit and implicit service promises are completely within a company's control. Managing these promises is a straightforward, sound approach for managing expectations. Yet many service organizations eschew this approach as evidenced by their penchant for overpromising as a way to entice customers. Our research revealed numerous instances of companies elevating customers' expectations to levels that would not be met. Comments made by a frustrated auto insurance customer are typical: "They say in their advertising that they are the 'good driver' company and yet my premiums kept going up even though I had no accidents. When I inquired they said it was because of the average number of accidents in my group."

Companies will benefit by making a concerted effort to ensure that their promises to customers reflect the actual service rather than an idealized, glorified version of it. Overpromising undermines customers' tolerance and trust. Customers' service expectations are really quite basic. Insurance customers want companies to pay up when there is a claim and provide some expertise for what is a complex service. Hotel customers want a clean, secure room and a smile from the staff. Repair customers want competent technicians to do the job right the first time. Exaggerated claims are unnecessary and harmful.

While our research revealed many disappointed service customers, extravagant expectations were seldom the source of their disappointment. Instead, the source frequently was customer distrust and intolerance spawned by inflated service claims, broken promises, and insufficient caring.

Lamenting the prevalence of complex promotional programs that are peripheral to the basic service, a hotel customer bemoaned: "I'd rather have no programs at all than have one that is supposed to benefit customers but actually aggravates them." A truck leasing customer voiced a similar sentiment: "These companies should establish a degree of continuity and concentrate on the service they are performing. They should get away from the trendy things."

Clearly, companies would do well to focus more on their basic services and present a cohesive, honest picture of those services both explicitly (e.g., advertising and personal selling) and implicitly (e.g., the appearance of service facilities, the price of the service). To ensure that the promised service is consistent with the deliverable service, managers should:

- Solicit pre-campaign feedback from front-line operations personnel and customers about the perceived accuracy of proposed promotional messages
- Devote greater attention to managing the service evidence (Chapter 6) to project accurate cues about the service
- Resist the urge to mimic competitors who fall prey to the temptation to overpromise
- Conduct periodic research to assess the influence of their prices on customers' expectation levels and price-value perceptions

PLACE A PREMIUM ON RELIABILITY

Performing the promised service right the first time—being reliable—directly contributes to service excellence because reliability is foremost to customers. However, being reliable also offers an important indirect benefit: it limits customers' expectations by reducing the need for recovery service. Service problems are transitory service intensifiers (Exhibit 4–3) that elevate customers' expectation levels during service recovery. A business-insurance customer made this point succinctly: "When foul-ups occur they drive up expectations because your 'awareness' goes up and tolerance goes down." When service problems occur, customers' tolerance zones typically shrink, and their adequate and desired service levels typically rise for both the outcome and process dimensions of the recovery service (Exhibit 4–5).

As discussed in Chapter 2, fostering a "do it right the first time" value system requires strong service leadership, thorough pre- and post-launch service testing, and an organizational "infrastructure"

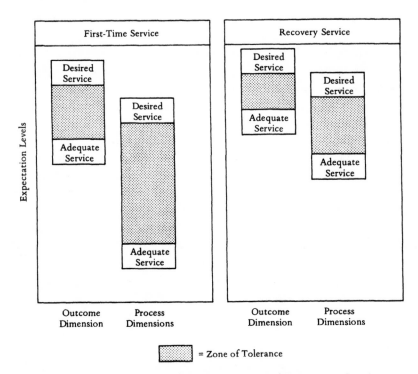

Exhibit 4–5 Tolerance Zones for First-Time and Recovery Service

(e.g., training, teamwork, reward systems) for error-free service. These three "pillars of support for service reliability" are also vital to managing customers' expectations effectively.

COMMUNICATE WITH CUSTOMERS

Regular communication with customers—to understand their expectations and concerns, to explain the service they receive, or simply to express appreciation for their business—encourages tolerance and, therefore, is a potent means for managing expectations. Our findings suggest that genuine communications that demonstrate a sense of caring widen customers' tolerance zones. As one business insurance customer said: "Insurance is a people business. If the insurance company talks to its customers and interacts with them effectively, a lot of the problems will go away."

Companies that strengthen customer ties through regular dialogue earn some goodwill chips to spend when problems occur. Mari Terbruegen, Vice President and Quality Service Officer at the Prudential Insurance Company, comments: "To manage a customer's expectations, the main ingredient is *communication*. . . . As long as customers know what to expect right from the start, as long as we stay in touch, there is little room for disappointment. . . . There's no reason to wait until customers have a specific problem or question to let them know we care about them. Through regular communication concerning things that affect them, many problems can be avoided and customer satisfaction can be increased."

Communicating with customers on a timely basis is an effective way of managing their expectations. Patients who receive a call from their doctor's office informing them that the doctor is running two hours late will have more realistic expectations—and show greater tolerance—than patients who learn of the delay after reaching the doctor's office. A bank that discovers an error in statements already mailed will have more tolerant customers if it immediately sends them a letter of apology and explanation than if it does not.

Proactive, company-initiated communications, and prompt, caring response to customer-initiated communications, convey a feeling of partnership that service customers frequently wish for but seldom experience. Communicating effectively with customers makes them feel appreciated and reduces or avoids frustration when service problems occur. Effective communications add value to what customers receive in return for what they pay, thereby fostering a perception of fair play and building customer trust and tolerance. Good customer communication is a cornerstone of relationship marketing, the subject of Chapter 8.

The ingredients for effectively communicating with customers and enlarging their tolerance zones include:

- Making company representatives easily accessible to customers
- Encouraging customers to contact the company —— ᴎ ᴄ
- Initiating contact with customers and following up regularly
- Training and facilitating employees to provide personalized, responsive, and caring service
- Rewarding employees for nurturing customer relationships

EXCEEDING CUSTOMERS' EXPECTATIONS

Managing expectations paves the way for exceeding them. In each focus group, we asked customers how companies could exceed their expectations. The following illustrative customer suggestions demonstrate the importance of effectively managing expectations—i.e., making realistic promises, being reliable, communicating regularly— for exceeding expectations:

AUTOMOBILE REPAIR CUSTOMER: Talk to your customers more. Be open and honest with customers.

AUTOMOBILE INSURANCE CUSTOMER: They don't have to do anything fancy. They should just make sure that everything goes the way it is supposed to go. That, in itself, will be a remarkable event and will "wow" me!

TRUCK LEASING CUSTOMER: Sometimes they take care of your problems too fast. They fix your truck and two days later you have to take it back for the same problem. They could be a little more attentive and fix the problem permanently.

HOTEL CUSTOMER: Acknowledge loyal customers. When employees remember and recognize you as a regular customer you feel really good.

BUSINESS EQUIPMENT REPAIR CUSTOMER: Show up sometimes when nothing is wrong.

BUSINESS INSURANCE CUSTOMER: It really boils down to communication . . . establishing a communication network both ways.

Failing to manage expectations is a principal cause of failing to exceed them. Managed expectations provide the base from which companies can capitalize on the opportunities that service delivery and recovery offer for exceeding customers' expectations.

EXCEL IN SERVICE DELIVERY

During service delivery, when customers directly experience providers' service skills and "tone," companies have the best opportunity to augment the service core of reliability in ways that differentiate one company from another. The lower expectations and wider tolerance zones that customers have for the service process dimensions (Exhibit 4–2) reflect the greater potential these dimensions hold for exceeding expectations. A hotel is unlikely to exceed a customer's expectations simply by having ready the customer's reserved, guaranteed room. This is what the hotel is supposed to do; there is no element of surprise. But with uncommon grace, courtesy, or caring, hotel employees can surprise customers and surpass their expectations.

When we asked customers what companies could do to exceed their expectations, virtually all of their responses concerned the service process. A business equipment repair customer suggested: "The service representative should be like a real person instead of just like a machine." A hotel customer said: "The one thing that will pick me up after being beat up all day is a smile and a warm welcome." An auto repair customer recommended: "Make the service department look better than a warehouse and more comfortable."

The service process also was prominent in respondents' narratives about service encounters that exceeded their expectations. For instance, an elated auto insurance customer said: "Something hit my car on the interstate. I called the 800 number and they took care of everything 'bam, bam, bam.' They gave me an adjuster and he was as friendly as he could be and told me to let him know if his adjustment wasn't enough."

Every customer contact is a potential opportunity to make the customer feel better than what experience has prepared him or her to expect. Alert employees who are well trained, encouraged, and motivated to excel in service delivery will capitalize on these opportunities. Apathetic employees who perform their jobs in robot-like fashion will waste the opportunities. Demonstrating service leadership (a topic touched on in Chapter 2) and preparing employees to interact well with customers (a subject covered in Chapter 3) are crucial for inspiring service personnel to be excellent servers. We elaborate on these topics and discuss additional guidelines for excelling on the process dimensions in subsequent chapters, especially Chapter 8 (marketing to existing customers) and Chapter 9 (marketing to employees).

CAPITALIZE ON SERVICE RECOVERY

Service recovery situations are golden opportunities for exceeding customers' expectations. Thomas R. Elsman, Strategic Planning Manager, Customer Service Division at DuPont, makes this point well: "As emergencies and complaints arise, deal with them with empathy and quick resolve, for outstanding service in this area will be viewed as going the extra mile and can turn a negative into a positive." Yet, as discussed in Chapter 3, many companies are ill-equipped for excelling in service recovery.

The process dimensions are especially important when dealing with service problems. While customers' expectations are higher for both the outcome and process dimensions during service recovery, the process dimensions provide greater opportunity for exceeding expectations (Exhibit 4–5). Moreover, as discussed in Chapter 3, customers are more attentive to the delivery process during recovery service than during routine service. The following answers given by focus group respondents when asked how companies could exceed expectations illustrate the pivotal role of the process dimensions in service recovery:

HOTEL CUSTOMER: Make you feel like they are really trying when they make a mistake. Say they'll do their best to help you . . . that's all it takes.

BUSINESS EQUIPMENT REPAIR CUSTOMER: Be more humane, helpful, and understanding. Realize that when you call with a problem you are in distress.

In Chapter 3 we discussed Toyota recalling 8,000 Lexus automobiles for repairs because of two customer complaints (one concerning a defective brake light and the other a sticky cruise-control mechanism). What was especially striking about this recall was that the Lexus dealers picked up, repaired, washed, and returned the cars to the owners. This story demonstrates the potential recovery situations hold for exceeding customers' expectations, nurturing customer relationships (Chapter 8), and stimulating positive word-of-mouth communications (Chapter 1).

Responsive, reassuring, and empathetic treatment of customers is most needed—but often absent—during recovery service. Recovery situations are thus opportune settings for pleasantly surprising customers and exceeding their expectations through exceptional service.

ESTABLISHING A CUSTOMER FRANCHISE

Insights about the structure and determinants of customer expectations emerging from our recent research provide a rich conceptual framework for evaluating a company's service quality and improving it to earn and strengthen customer loyalty. Based on earlier research, we have developed an approach for quantifying customers' service quality assessments as the gap between their perceptions and expectations.[6] Because our latest research suggests that customers' service expectations exist at both adequate and desired levels, ideally *two* potential service quality gaps should be assessed: the gap between perceived service and adequate service, and the gap between perceived service and desired service. We label the former *measure of service adequacy* (MSA) and the latter *measure of service superiority* (MSS) and define them as follows:

MSA = Perceived Service minus Adequate Service
MSS = Perceived Service minus Desired Service

A company's MSA and MSS scores will determine its competitive position from a service quality standpoint. As Exhibit 4–6 shows, depending on the relative levels of customer perceptions and expectations, a company can operate at a competitive disadvantage, a competitive advantage, or at the customer franchise level in terms of its service.

The adequate service level reflects the *minimum* performance level expected by customers after they consider a variety of personal and external factors (Exhibit 4–3), including the availability of alternative service options. Companies whose service performance falls short of this level are at a competitive disadvantage, with the disadvantage escalating as the gap widens. These companies' customers may well be "reluctant" customers, ready to take their business elsewhere the moment they perceive a viable service alternative.

Exhibit 4–6 Relative Competitive Status Defined by Measures of Service Adequacy and Superiority

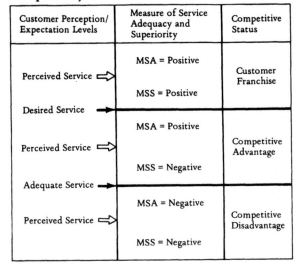

Customer Perception/ Expectation Levels	Measure of Service Adequacy and Superiority	Competitive Status
Perceived Service ⇒ Desired Service →	MSA = Positive / MSS = Positive	Customer Franchise
Perceived Service ⇒ Adequate Service →	MSA = Positive / MSS = Negative	Competitive Advantage
Perceived Service ⇒	MSA = Negative / MSS = Negative	Competitive Disadvantage

Companies must perform *above* the adequate service level to use service quality for competitive advantage. A favorable MSA score, however, may signal only a temporary advantage. Customers' adequate service levels, which our research suggests are less stable than the desired service levels, will rise rapidly when competitors promise and deliver a higher level of service. If a company's MSA score is barely positive to begin with, a competitively induced elevation in the adequate service level will nullify the company's competitive advantage (i.e., turn the MSA score from positive to negative and plunge the firm into competitive disadvantage). Thus, companies currently performing in the region of competitive advantage can ill afford complacency. To consolidate their competitive advantage and to reduce their vulnerability to upward surges in the adequate service level, these companies should strive to augment their positive MSA scores and decrease the deficiency in their MSS scores.

To develop a true customer franchise (i.e., *unwavering* customer loyalty), companies must exceed not only the adequate service level but also the desired service level. Exceptional service can intensify customers' loyalty to a point where they virtually "tune out" competitive options. A hotel customer's experience illustrates: "I left my portfolio on top of a cab. The hotel broke its neck to get it back to me. Now, whenever I go to Chicago I stay at that same hotel."

Companies must conduct periodic research to monitor customers' expectations, to understand the specific factors driving them, and to assess service performance against them.[7] Information generated by such research will be valuable in devising effective strategies for managing and exceeding expectations, thereby turning service quality into a powerful competitive weapon. Continuous striving for service superiority—consistently performing above the adequate service level and capitalizing on every opportunity to exceed the desired service level—is essential for establishing a customer franchise.

SUMMARY AND ACTION CHECKLIST

Customers' expectations are the true standards for judging service quality. Understanding the nature and determinants of expectations is essential for ensuring that service performance meets or exceeds expectations.

Customers have two levels of expectations—adequate and desired service—separated by a zone of tolerance. The expectation levels, and hence the zone of tolerance, can vary across customers and across service encounters in response to a variety of personal and external factors. In general, customers tend to have higher expectation levels and narrower tolerance zones for the service outcome dimension of reliability than for the service process dimensions of tangibles, responsiveness, assurance, and empathy. Also, expectations are likely to be higher, and tolerance zones smaller, during recovery service than during first-time service.

Effectively managing expectations sets the stage for surpassing them, which, in turn, contributes to cultivating a customer franchise. We propose the following action checklist for fostering customer loyalty through managing and exceeding expectations:

1. *Do we strive to present a realistic picture of our service to customers?* Do we always check the accuracy of our promotional messages prior to customers' exposure to them? Is there regular communication between employees who serve customers and those who make promises to customers? Do we assess the impact on customer expectations of cues such as price?

2. *Is performing the service right the first time a top priority in our company?* Do we stress to our employees that providing

reliable service is an effective way of managing customers' expectations? Are our employees trained and rewarded for delivering error-free service? Do we regularly evaluate our service designs to identify and correct potential flaws?

3. *Do we communicate effectively with customers?* Do we periodically contact customers to ascertain their needs and appreciate their business? Do we train and require employees to demonstrate to customers we care about and value them?

4. *Do we surprise customers during the service process?* Are our employees aware that the process of service delivery represents the prime opportunity to *exceed* customers' expectations? Do we take specific steps to encourage excellence during service delivery?

5. *Do our employees regard service problems as opportunities to impress customers, or as annoyances?* Do we prepare and encourage employees to excel in the service recovery *process?* Do we reward them for providing exceptional recovery service?

6. *Do we continuously evaluate and improve our performance against customers' expectations?* Do we perform consistently above the adequate service level? Do we capitalize on opportunities to exceed the desired service level?

Building a Services Marketing Organization

5

◇◇◇

Turning Marketing
into a Line Function

E xcellent service is the foundation for excellent services marketing. When service is excellent, marketing is easier. Price hikes
are more palatable because customers perceive value in the service.
The advertising conflicts less with the reality of service delivery—
and benefits from the reinforcement of positive word-of-mouth communications. Sales personnel have confidence in the services and thus
sell them more vigorously.

Aggressively marketing a low-quality service undercuts a firm's future. More customers are tempted to try the service—or to try it
again—only to discover firsthand that they have made a mistake.
Now what does the firm do? The theme of this book is that high-
performance services marketing begins and ends with excellent service. Quality service is the essence, the core, of services marketing.

Because services are performances rather than manufactured ob-
jects, and because these performances often require the physical presence of the customer, and because these performances are frequently
rendered by human beings, the significant opportunity for services
marketing exists in the field where service provider and customer
interact. It is in the field where equipment repair technicians respond
to service calls, where walk-in clinic physicians treat patients, where
department store salespeople show dresses to consumers. It is in the
field where the company either lives up to its advertising promises
or breaks them, earns its price or destroys pricing credibility, cross-
sells other services or simply takes orders, strengthens customer relationships or chases customers away.

That services marketing depends on service quality and occurs primarily in the field holds important implications for what staff marketing directors in service firms should do, what kind of people should be in these positions, and what CEOs must do to support these people. These issues are the focus of this chapter.

CORNERSTONE ROLES
FOR THE MARKETING DIRECTOR

In service businesses the least effective marketing department executives strive to be clever marketers; the most effective executives strive to turn everyone else in the organization into clever marketers. *In service businesses the most effective staff marketing directors turn marketing into a line function.* Their philosophy is helping the organization to become a marketing institution, rather than doing the marketing for the organization.

Tom Fitzgerald, Vice President of Corporate Marketing for ARA Services, an international, diversified service company with more than $4 billion in sales, is on target when he states:

> The principal challenge for service company marketing executives is recognizing that most of the traditional marketing functions are really the responsibility of someone else in the organization—primarily what we call "operations."
>
> The role of the marketing department in service companies then becomes more of a supportive one facilitating the process of *ensuring the business is focused on its markets.*

Here is what Fitzgerald advises services marketing directors to do:

1. Determine the level of the "marketing mentality" in your business. You may have to generate a complete change in culture or simply do some fine-tuning.

2. Integrate your marketing orientation into operations by developing a combined "business plan" (which includes marketing) rather than a separate "marketing plan"—this helps unify the organization rather than dividing it.

3. Don't try to create a large, separate marketing department. A services business needs only a few marketing specialists who understand the operations culture and who will help keep the organization focused on the customer.

In service businesses, small marketing departments are more beautiful than large ones, and an *essential* commitment for staff marketing executives is to help build a marketing mentality throughout the organization. Staff executives who do not approach the task of services marketing in this way are priming the company's marketing—and themselves—for failure.

A marketing mentality is like a garden of customer-responsive strategies, attitudes, habits, skills, knowledge, systems, and tools that exist in an organization at any time. With the proper attention and nurturing the plants flourish; without these, the garden will die.

The marketing director is responsible for making the marketing garden flourish. He or she does not need a big entourage or fancy trappings to do this; indeed, that just gets in the way. What the director does need is a bold vision of what the garden can be and a strong commitment to keeping the garden healthy and growing during all seasons.

The marketing director has three key leadership roles to perform in helping to build and sustain a marketing institution. These roles are ongoing—changing in degree but not kind—as the firm's marketing mentality evolves. (For some thoughts on the key roles of the CEO in supporting the marketing director's mandate, see Exhibit 5–1).

ROLE ONE: CHANGE ARCHITECT

The fundamental idea of marketing is effecting a good fit between the organization and its markets. As its markets change, so must the organization. Nothing is forever in the marketing environment. Not cultural values. Not demographics. Not the economy. Not technologies. Not competition. Not the political climate.

A key role for service firm marketing directors is to help redefine their institutions' strategic directions in response to changing market conditions. Market-sensitive strategic change is at the heart of organizational renewal. Good examples of this are the Girl Scouts of the U.S.A. shifting focus from preparing young girls for homemaking to preparing them for careers, and JC Penney transforming itself from an eclectic general merchandise chain to a fashion department store chain for middle-scale consumers.

Marketing directors need to help renew their institutions before it is too late. To do this they must contribute to the architecture for change. Two blueprints are needed—one that defines a strategic di-

Exhibit 5-1 How the CEO Can Support the Marketing Director

Leading marketing executives were asked to indicate the single most important action a CEO can take in helping the services marketing director to be successful. Here are their answers:

Participation! The Marketing Director must be a full and equal participant in the key business discussions of the organization. Good business decisions need to be based on more than "executive research" (i.e., what I and my mother-in-law think) and pure financial analysis. The Marketing Director is the channel to market research, customer views, sales issues, competitive analysis, and product delivery issues. The CEO must see that the Director is given the opportunity to express his/her views and influence outcomes. Then it's up to the Director to be a well-prepared, effective professional.

— Leslie R. Butler
Vice Chairman
First Pennsylvania Bank

I believe the single most important action a CEO can take in helping insure marketing program success is to make sure that marketing perspectives and issues are well represented on strategic meeting agendas. This develops a common organizational understanding of programs, which ultimately leads to crisp, efficient execution.

— Dick Hammill
Vice President—Marketing
and Advertising
The Home Depot, Inc.

The CEO of a services firm must be the central focus for establishing the corporation's positioning objective so that it reflects what senior management believes is the company's strategic customer advantage. This will permit the marketing director to create a brand "ownership" that sufficiently differentiates the products and services from those of the competition which will, in turn, provide the basis for establishing a brand preference in the mind of the customer.

— Charles J. Ferrero
Senior Vice President
Midlantic National Bank

Service providers are inveterate scorekeepers. They search for clear and consistent signs of what's really important to their CEOs. Their action as well as their analytical, interpersonal and creative skills are channeled by leadership example and by what gets recognized and rewarded. The right organizational chain reactions occur in a services firm whenever the CEO reinforces legendary service wherever it can be found — and in myriad planned and spontaneous ways. Memorable happenings influence future behavior. That means a CEO's on-the-spot words of praise, support of performance team suggestions, commitment to bonus awards and gain-sharing for exceeding customer service targets, and attendance at team celebrations are strong organizational stuff.

— George A. Rieder
President
George A. Rieder Associates, Inc.

Exhibit 5-1 Continued

> The single most important thing a CEO can do to help a services firm marketing director be successful is to constantly reinforce the significance of marketing and client service throughout the organization.
>
> PHH Corporation CEO Bob Kunisch takes every opportunity to talk to employees about the PHH Quality Service Promise and his vision of a totally customer-focused environment at PHH. He emphasizes that everyone at PHH is in marketing, with key roles to play in delivering our quality commitments.
>
> In addition to reinforcing the quality message internally, Bob spends about 25% of his time visiting clients and prospects. This personal involvement demonstrates to clients that Bob truly lives, breathes and practices the PHH Quality Service Promise.
>
> — Gene Arbaugh
> Corporate Vice President-
> Marketing
> PHH Corporation

rection that will be relevant and profitable in the years ahead, and another that presents the internal strategies needed to actually change the institution. Effective change-making requires both an external strategy (what the organization is to become) *and* an internal strategy (how to pave the way for change). Marketing directors need to work with line executives in formulating both types of strategies.

ROLE TWO: MARKETING FACILITATOR

Service firm marketing directors need to capitalize on the reality that employees performing the services are closest to the customer; they are in the best position to be marketers. A primary role of the marketing director is to facilitate the process of in-the-field, service provider-to-customer marketing.

Packaged goods marketers "push" the trade and "pull" the consumer to market their wares. "Push" and "pull" marketing applies to services as well but with several important twists. Services marketing directors need to push and pull employees performing services so that they will want to be—and know how to be—effective marketers.

Just as packaged goods marketers have two sets of customers (the trade and the end-customer), so do services marketers (the employee service provider and the end-customer). In effect, the firm's own service providers are the equivalent of wholesale and retail distributors in packaged goods marketing. Service employees are the critical *linkage* between the marketing department and the end-customer. These employees are the conduit through which marketing either realizes its potential or does not. As one of us wrote in an early paper on this idea: "Services marketing directors not only must persuade customers to buy, they must also persuade—and help—employees to perform."[1]

Marketing directors can facilitate marketing throughout the organization in at least three ways. *First, they can work continuously to educate managerial and nonmanagerial employees about the nature, purposes, and applications of marketing.* Employees cannot be expected to have a marketing mentality if they do not understand what marketing is. The most effective services marketing directors devote considerable time and resources to one-on-one education, to sponsoring or supporting marketing seminars and training courses, and to getting the right reading material on marketing to the right people.

Listen to Les Butler, Vice Chairman of First Pennsylvania Bank in Philadelphia, on the subject of marketing director as educator:

> Part of the job of the marketing director is that of educator. Saying that a company should be market driven is not enough. Suggesting the use of well-structured research to address an issue is not enough. The marketing director must teach marketing to his or her customers (the line organization). Many line managers lack marketing backgrounds, they are busy people, and they are prone (rewarded even) to relying on gut instincts or "feeling." The marketing director has to reexamine the obligation to teach, to champion, to preach the marketing discipline and to reinforce that message.

Second, marketing directors need to strive to make it easier for employees to practice marketing. The best marketing directors focus on giving employees the tools they need to be effective marketers. These executives involve themselves in helping to create, for example:

- Customer information files that contact employees can use to better understand their customers' needs
- Operating systems that speed routine transactions and free employees for cross-selling
- Internal training and communication services so employees can be more competent and feel more confident with customers

The best marketing directors understand that services marketing effectiveness is a direct function of employees' *willingness* and *ability* to engage in marketing behavior at the point of sale and delivery.

This seems like such an obvious point. Our experience indicates that the obvious in services marketing is often overlooked. Anna Kahn, a services marketing consultant in Stockholm, Sweden, draws a similar conclusion:

> The marketing directors in Swedish service companies still underestimate the needs of employee training before they introduce a service to the external market. Low scores are very common when you ask the employees about the training before the launch of a new service. Not only training is necessary, but also a process to make the employees accept the service to the extent that they want to be the first consumers of the service themselves.

Third, the marketing director must be a relentless, visible champion for quality service in the organization. Other than the CEO, no one in the firm has more at stake in the service quality journey than the marketing director. As we have stressed, excellent service makes every other facet of services marketing more potent and poor service makes every other facet less potent.

The marketing director must:

- Be an advocate for service excellence inside the company
- Help show the way in the organization to improved service
- Assess the impact on service quality of *all* marketing decisions—ensuring that these decisions support quality improvement rather than undermine it

Because quality service is the core of services marketing, the marketing director must be a key player in a firm's strategic efforts to improve quality. By helping the firm improve its quality, the marketing director facilitates marketing. If the firm has a service quality steering council, the marketing director should be a member. If the firm has a separate "quality" department, then this department and the marketing department need to work together closely.

To think of services marketing and service quality as two independent functions or disciplines is to deny the reality that they are inseparable. Without quality service, the rest of what we label as "services marketing" will be ineffective and thus irrelevant.

ROLE THREE: IMAGE MANAGER

Still another critical role for services marketing directors is institutional image management. Helping the company to fit its environment and facilitating marketing effectiveness at the point of customer contact contribute directly to a positive company image. Nonetheless, the intangibility of services challenges the services marketer to use all possible means to establish a distinctive and compelling company identity.

Competing airlines often fly the same types of planes to and from the same airports about the same time of day or night while regularly matching each others' fares and special promotions. With the airlines—and with numerous other service industries—the tangibles supporting the invisible service are quite similar and competitive differentiation is a problem. Transforming similarity into distinctiveness is no small task when the product is a performance.

John Hamby, President of the Glastonbury Bank and Trust Company in Glastonbury, Connecticut, captures the image challenge in services marketing:

> Differentiating oneself from the competition, both in fact and in the eyes of customers and prospective customers, is one of the persistent challenges in our business. Nothing works quite as well as having superior answers to meet the needs of the customer. However, even when one can achieve product superiority there remains the problem in service businesses of making sure the difference is recognized and applauded.

Services marketers need to take full advantage of whatever competitive advantages a firm might have by communicating these differences cohesively, consistently, and strikingly. Required is a strategic and proactive approach to defining clearly a company's special competencies—its "reason for being"—through communications media. Required are services marketing directors who strive to brand the company, not just specific services the company sells; who realize that everything sensory associated with a company communicates something; and who thus attempt to mobilize all of these stimuli into one powerful message.

THE IDEAL SERVICES MARKETING DIRECTOR

The cornerstone roles of the services firm marketing director clearly suggest the kind of person needed to assume these roles. Few staffing decisions are as critical as choosing the marketing director, given the strategic, culture-shaping, and corporate communication roles this person must play. The marketing director's position is not a position on which to pinch pennies. The best services marketing directors have true leadership capabilities, are tuned into the differences between goods and services marketing, are knowledgeable about the industry in which they work, and have excellent teaching skills.

MARKETING LEADERSHIP AND OTHER TRAITS

The best marketing directors have leadership qualities. They have the strategic vision to help their companies respond to changing market conditions, and they have the interpersonal skills to cajole, persuade, inspire, and sometimes push others in the organization toward the vision.

Top-notch services marketers have what consultant/writer Barry Deutsch calls "creative unreasonableness." They strive to be responsive to the line organization without compromising the strategic and executional requirements of excellent marketing. Here is how Deutsch describes the challenge:

> Learning when to be reasonable and when to be unreasonable is the most difficult task of all. What we are talking about is the constant necessity to balance responsiveness to the organization with leadership.
>
> . . . The standouts are those who lead their organization, sometimes against the collective will, to be a stronger force in markets. . . . The standouts are unreasonable when confronted with an organization determined to be good enough instead of as good as it can be.[2]

Sensitivity to the nuances of *services* marketing is also critical. Many executives experienced in goods marketing have struggled or failed outright in making the transition to services marketing. With services there is nothing to market but the service. Goods marketers market "things" that employees distant from customers make; almost all of the marketing occurs *outside* the factory. Services marketers market intangible "performances" by employees who frequently interact with customers; much of the marketing occurs *inside* the "factory." Here again are the words of Swedish consultant Anna Kahn:

> Today everyone knows the differences between goods and services and still it very often happens that services are marketed

in the same way as goods. Services are bought on the basis of confidence in the people who produce them and in their qualifications. Relationship marketing and networking are the most important ways of marketing services. The more complicated the service, the more important it is to create confidence in the people producing the service.

Knowledge of the industry is another important characteristic of services marketing directors. Marketing directors need to "know the business" to help develop the proper strategies and to earn the necessary respect within the organization to ensure their implementation. Marketing directors should be just as knowledgeable about competitors, just as conversant with legislative and regulatory trends, just as interested in relevant industry technology, as any senior line executive in the company. And no one in the company should know more about the customer than the marketing director. Superficial knowledge of the business undermines the strategic thinking and personal credibility integral to the marketing director's leadership.

Finally, the best marketing directors have the "soul of a teacher." Knowing services marketing and knowing the business is not enough; the marketing director must also be able to "market" marketing to the line organization. Education is crucial. Understanding precedes commitment. An individual who lacks the skills and desire to educate managerial and nonmanagerial personnel about the nature, value, and applications of marketing will fail in the services marketing director position.

AN INTUITIVE SERVICES MARKETER

Gene Arbaugh, Vice President of Corporate Marketing for PHH Corporation, a *Fortune 500* services company whose subsidiaries market asset and financial management services for corporate and government customers, exemplifies the characteristics we have discussed. Arbaugh came to his current position from the presidency of PHH's largest subsidiary, Peterson, Howell and Heather (now known as PHH FleetAmerica), which offers automobile and truck fleet management services.

Arbaugh knows the fleet management and other PHH businesses inside and out. Trained as a lawyer, Arbaugh is analytical and precise in the way he approaches any task. He is as "numbers oriented" as any member of senior management, and he has not been ensnared in the imagery of "bottom-line softness" that victimizes many marketing directors.

Although PHH Corporation is a $2 billion business, Arbaugh has a tiny staff; he knows that the action is in the line organizations and that his job is to help them practice marketing more successfully. Working closely with his CEO, Robert Kunisch, Arbaugh has focused his energies on helping the PHH companies make the cultural shift from an independent, operations focus to an interdependent, customer focus. Each year Arbaugh offers internal education events that bring together senior and middle executives from the various operating companies so that they can learn more about the other PHH businesses, forge bonds of teamwork, and develop a deeper sense of PHH as one company instead of many independent companies. Arbaugh's annual one-week marketing course for company executives rivals any such course in the United States in terms of the "all-star" cast of professors who are hired to teach it.

Arbaugh's cross-marketing initiative in which employees of one PHH company are rewarded for selling the services of another is the institutionalized form of a process made possible by the movement toward a one-company culture. The cross-marketing initiative also is aided by Arbaugh's constant emphasis on improved service quality—so employees in one PHH company will be willing to "risk" their customers to another.

A smart services marketer, Arbaugh markets continuously *to* the PHH organization. He states:

> Make every employee in your corporation a marketer of your services. Through our Sharing Leads Bonus Program, we will pay a bonus to *any* and *all* employees who give us a lead that results in our obtaining a signed contract. We promote this activity through an employee newsletter which gives information on the services we offer, gives recognition to the people who have provided us successful leads, and continually reinforces that every employee is in marketing.
>
> Recently, one of our secretaries submitted leads which resulted in two large contracts; and company-wide, we are now signing millions of dollars worth of new business annually due to this program.

Arbaugh's senior-level line experience and his ability to talk "numbers" with the number-crunchers give him the organizational entree that is his lifeblood in the marketing director's chair. His sincerity and responsive attitude help him to sustain that entree. His staff, small as it is, is first-rate. Arbaugh also has the self-confidence to shine the spotlight on the field organizations, rather than on himself or others at headquarters. He prefers to work behind the scenes, smoothing out trouble spots, making a key telephone call or jumping on an airplane to bring a defecting client back into the fold.

Arbaugh is a patient man who accepts the slow, painstaking, two-steps-forward, one-step-backward reality of changing a corporate culture. From day one of assuming his post as corporate marketing director, Arbaugh clearly saw the potential of using a common brand name to bring together under one marketing umbrella such disparate company names as Homequity, U.S. Mortgage, and Fantus. Numerous customers and customer-prospects had no idea that these and other companies were PHH companies, and some had never heard of PHH Corporation.

Many marketing directors would have jumped on the branding opportunity, making it one of their first priorities. Arbaugh instead bided his time, realizing the sensitivity of this issue in the field organizations and understanding that internal change needed to precede external change. He has been deliberate on this issue, encouraging the use of PHH in combination with the existing name, e.g., PHH Homequity.

Gene Arbaugh is an intuitive services marketer. Although he lacks formal collegiate education in marketing, he nevertheless understands the critical distinction between the marketing department and the marketing function in a service business. Arbaugh's singular commitment to helping members of the line organization become better marketers is the key to his success.

SUMMARY AND ACTION CHECKLIST

In service businesses, the most successful marketing directors are those who turn line employees on to marketing and who help them to be successful in this role. The best marketing directors seek to capitalize when service production occurs at the point of sale. The central question is: If I have dozens (or hundreds or thousands) of service producers interacting with customers during the production/delivery process, what can I do to transform them into marketers, too? What can I do to enhance their willingness and ability to answer customers' questions knowledgeably and gracefully; to respond to customers' legitimate, nonroutine needs with a sense of urgency; to learn the features and benefits of our range of services and to cross-sell these services proactively? The most effective services marketing directors attempt to transform *every* employee into a marketer. This is the magic of Gene Arbaugh, who has secretaries submitting sales leads.

Playing a leadership role in building and sustaining a marketing mentality in the organization is but one of three interrelated roles for the services firm marketing director. The marketing director must also help blueprint the firm's strategic future—its businesses, market offers, and marketing methods—and the firm's mechanisms for internal change.

If the marketing director is not centrally involved in helping to define the firm's strategic future, he or she is less likely to be effective in leading the cultural transformation required for the firm to become something new.

The third role is the corporate communications role—finding ways to overcome the marketing drawbacks of product intangibility, finding ways to turn customers' vague impressions into sharp, distinct images. Here again is a role that requires a broad strategic perspective in which pieces of a communications puzzle are fitted together into a cohesive and powerful whole. As with the other two roles, the tactical approach is insufficient.

The services marketing director's three roles build on one another: mapping out an agenda for change, nurturing a marketing mentality among employees so that the firm can realize its future promise, communicating the firm's identity and strengths in such a way that the firm becomes distinctive among its publics.

The roles of a services marketing director suggest the following action checklist for individuals in this position:

1. *Am I on the cutting edge of change in my business?* Am I staying abreast of changing markets, technologies, competitors, and legislative/regulatory patterns?

2. *Do we have a company blueprint for what we wish to be?* Do we have a second blueprint on how we will actually move the company in the new directions? Did I play an active role in developing these blueprints? If not, why not and what should I do differently in the future?

3. *Am I actively teaching marketing in the organization?* Should I and others who are particularly marketing-minded be more

involved in our company's regular training programs? Should I create one or more marketing courses to be taught inside our company? Should I be more aggressive in inviting our key executives to attend outside marketing courses or conferences? Can I more productively use learning technology to educate more employees more of the time? Should I establish a company marketing library?

4. *Am I doing enough to facilitate marketing within the organization?* Am I devoting most of my professional time and departmental resources to helping employees be more effective marketers? If not, what am I doing with my time and these resources that is more important?

5. *Am I listening to my internal customers—managers and nonmanagers alike?* Do I know what obstacles block their way to better marketing? Do I know what is making them less willing and/or less able to be the marketers I want them to be? Am I doing everything possible to remove these obstacles?

6. *Am I in the forefront in this company's efforts to improve service quality?* Am I providing the kind of leadership that quality improvement demands? Am I and the rest of the marketing department setting a good example in terms of the quality of service we offer? Am I making the extra effort on the investments that are imperative—for example, installing an ongoing service quality measurement system? Am I sufficiently sensitive to the potentially adverse effects on quality from marketing decisions we make in the organization? Am I taking appropriate action when conflicts are identified?

7. *Am I dealing with the branding opportunity comprehensively and strategically?* Am I blending all of our communication opportunities into a cohesive message? Is our message compelling? Do our key publics view us as different from the competition, and, if so, in what way? What else can I do to strengthen our branding?

8. *Am I pushing marketing down into the line organization where it belongs?* Am I pushing hard enough? Am I writing marketing plans or am I helping line executives write marketing plans? Am I developing new services, or am I helping line executives develop new services? Am I keeping my department small enough to still convey the message that marketing is a line function?

Maximizing Services Marketing Potential

6

◇◇◇

Managing the Evidence

Services differ fundamentally from goods by their intangibility. A good is in essence an object, a thing. A service in essence is a performance. The nonphysical nature of a service has important implications for how service customers form impressions and make buying decisions, and how services marketers approach the marketing task.

G. Lynn Shostack, one of America's most respected thinkers in the services field, states, "A physical object is self-defining; a service is not."[1] Shostack captures a crucial challenge in high performance services marketing: defining for the service what the service cannot define for itself. Customers cannot see a service, but they can see various tangibles associated with the service. They see service facilities, equipment, employees, communication materials, other customers, and price lists, among other things. All of these tangibles are "clues" about the invisible service.

Because customers must try to understand a service without actually seeing it, because they want to know what they are buying and why they should buy *before* making a purchase decision, they tend to be especially attentive to tangible clues about the service. For better or for worse, these tangible clues do communicate. If unmanaged, the clues can convey all the wrong messages about the service, seriously undermining the overall marketing strategy. If well-managed, the clues can teach customers about the service, bringing vitality and reinforcement to the marketing strategy.

The question is not whether service customers will perceive tangible clues about the service; most customers, most of the time, will. The question is whether they will perceive managed or unmanaged clues. The question is: will customers experience the marketer's intended or unintended evidence?

93

The concept of managing the evidence is not new. In 1973, Kotler wrote about "atmospherics" as a marketing tool, proposing "the conscious designing of space to create certain effects in buyers."[2] Shostack introduced the term "managing the evidence" in 1977 when she wrote:

> Product marketing tends to give first emphasis to creating *abstract* associations. *Service* marketers, on the other hand, should be focused on enhancing and differentiating "realities" through manipulation of *tangible* clues. The management of evidence comes first for service marketers. . . .[3]

Berry underscored the message in 1980 when he wrote, "A prime responsibility for the service marketer is to manage . . . tangibles so that the proper signals are conveyed about the service."[4] In 1985 Upah and Fulton introduced the term "Situation Creation," by which they mean designing the physical environment to nurture the desired attitudes and behavior during the service encounter.[5]

Why devote a full chapter in a book on high performance services marketing in the 1990s to a concept that has been written about in the marketing literature for two decades? One reason is that this is a *central* concept in services marketing. If this were a book on packaged goods marketing, this would be the packaging chapter. Just as toothpaste or frozen food packages communicate the product inside, so do tangibles associated with a service tell a story about it.

A second reason for this chapter is our interest in extending the evidence management topic. Most existing literature on this subject focuses on service facilities as evidence. We do the same, but we also suggest other types of evidence and discuss a broader range of applications for this concept. We use the existing literature as a springboard for new explorations.

TYPES OF EVIDENCE

What evidence do customers use to better understand the service? What evidence should marketers be managing? We propose three categories of evidence as shown in Exhibit 6–1: the physical environment, communications, and prices. The categories are not mutually exclusive, as indicated by the linked circles. For example, prices represent a different class of evidence than either physical facilities or

Exhibit 6-1 Types of Evidence

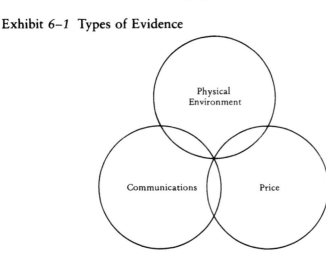

persuasive communications, yet they are communicated through various media inside and away from the service environment.

THE PHYSICAL ENVIRONMENT

Julie Baker, a graduate of Texas A&M University's doctoral program in marketing and a former environmental design student, has developed a useful paradigm to illustrate the nature and importance of physical facilities where services are delivered. Her framework, shown in Exhibit 6-2, breaks the physical environment into three basic categories: ambient factors, design factors, and social factors.[6]

Ambient Factors. Ambient factors are background conditions that exist below the level of immediate awareness and typically draw attention only when absent or unpleasant. Air temperature and noise levels are examples. Because ambient factors usually are taken for granted, their influence is typically neutral or negative. In other words, customer awareness of ambient factors more likely provokes avoidance behavior than approach behavior. For example, a customer avoids a certain restaurant because it is "noisy."

Design Factors. Design factors are visual stimuli that are far more likely to be apparent to customers than ambient factors. Accordingly, design factors have a comparatively greater potential for producing positive customer perceptions and encouraging approach behavior. Design factors can be classified as either aesthetic (e.g., architecture,

Exhibit 6-2 Components of the Physical Environment

Ambient Factors	Background conditions that exist below the level of a customer's immediate awareness	• Air Quality
		  • Temperature
		  • Humidity
		  • Circulation/
		    Ventilation
		• Noise
		• Scent
		• Cleanliness

Design Factors*	Stimuli that exist at the forefront of a customer's awareness	Aesthetic • Architecture • Color • Scale • Materials • Texture/Pattern • Shape • Style • Accessories Functional • Layout • Comfort • Signage
Social Factors	People in the environment	Audience (other customers) • Number • Appearance • Behavior Service Personnel • Number • Appearance • Behavior

*Interior and exterior.

SOURCE: Adapted from Julie Baker, "The Role of the Environment in Marketing Services: The Consumer Perspective," in John A Czepiel, Carole Congram and James Shanahan, eds., *The Service Challenge: Integrating for Competitive Advantage* (Chicago: American Marketing Association, 1987), p. 80.

color) or functional (e.g., layout, comfort). Design factors apply to both the exterior and interior of service facilities.

A service company that manages the design factors well is Sewell Village Cadillac in Dallas, one of America's most successful Cadillac dealerships. Unlike the garish, overstated appearance of many automobile dealerships, Sewell Village Cadillac's physical environment is in tune with its target market. Manicured lawns, trees, a spacious driveway and canopy at the showroom entrance, and tasteful signage signal elegance and classiness from the outside. Once inside the showroom, visitors find carpeting with the Cadillac wreath and crest woven into it, oak paneling throughout, leather-upholstered chairs, three Williamsburg chandeliers, and an enormous vase filled with fresh flowers. Covering the bathroom walls is expensive wallpaper; hanging on these walls are framed prints. The floors in the service departments are scrubbed nightly. The sanding equipment used in the body shop even has an attached vacuum hose that captures the dust before it hits the floor.[7]

The service departments at Sewell Village are kept so clean that they offer a sharp, visual contrast to what customers usually experience at auto dealerships and emit clues that communicate high standards of service and workmanship. In his book, *Customers for Life,* company president Carl Sewell writes:

> Disney World is the image we keep in mind when we're thinking about how our stores should look. We make sure the grass is always cut. I picked out every tree and bush. And we make sure the buildings are freshly painted. We try to keep the place, both inside and out, immaculate. (We even bought a street sweeper so that we'd be able to clean the roads in front of our dealerships.) . . . How we decorate and present our store . . . says a lot about the way we feel about our customers and employees.[8]

Social Factors. Social factors refer to the human component of the physical environment—customers and service personnel. The number, appearance, and behavior of customers and employees in the service environment can induce either approach or avoidance behavior, depending on the service expectations of a given customer. A convenience food store in New York received national publicity in 1990 for management's creative solution to the problem of rowdy teenagers "hanging out" in the parking lot. The store manager installed exterior loudspeakers and played "adult" music through them. Hating the music, the teenagers quickly found a different to congregate. The store manager had a problem with social f undermining the intended image for his store, and he took a change the evidence.

The appearance of service employees is especially crit dence management because customers typically do no between the service and the service provider. To the customer, a disheveled waiter is a disheveled restaurant. This is the point Professor Michael Solomon makes when he writes about "people packaging":

> The presentation of the product is crucial—the only difference [in services] is that since the product is largely people, it must be people who are correctly packaged. . . . An accountant wearing a loud suit, a *maitre d'hotel* in jeans, or a female executive in an alluring dress will rarely inspire the trust required to carry out his/her duties. The individual is trying to communicate a certain image; his/her clothing stands as a tangible contradiction.[9]

No company is better at managing the appearance of service personnel than Walt Disney World. All theme park personnel who meet the public (known as "on-stage cast members" at Disney) wear freshly cleaned costumes each day. They enter their stations from an underground staging facility (think of it as the "understage") and thus are *never* out of theme. Disney has the strictest personal grooming standards for service employees (some would say "old-fashioned strict") that we have ever encountered in our studies. Acceptable hair length, jewelry and makeup use, and other personal grooming factors are precisely defined and strictly enforced by Disney.

Some observers disagree with Disney's inflexibility. We would argue that Disney's ability to field neatly groomed, unfailingly cheerful, well-trained "cast members" is essential to creating a fantasyland that as many as 150,000 guests a day pay a premium price to experience. It is not magic that creates the Magic Kingdom; it is the grind of hard work and zealous attention to managing the smallest of tangible clues.

COMMUNICATIONS

Communications are another form of evidence about the service. These communications come from the company itself and from other interested parties; they are delivered in a variety of media and convey much about the service—for better or for worse. From billing statements to advertising, from customer word-of-mouth communications to company signage, from membership cards to personal selling, these various communications send clues about the service, either the right or the wrong ones. They reinforce the firm's marketing strategy or scramble it in hopeless confusion.

⸻ice companies that effectively manage communications do so

by emphasizing existing evidence and by creating new evidence. They make both the service and the message more tangible. Exhibit 6–3 provides an overview of the approaches service companies can use to manage the evidence through communications.

Tangibilizing the Service. Sometimes it is possible to make the service more physical and, therefore, less abstract. One technique is to *emphasize in communications tangibles associated with the service as though they were the service.* Firms using this technique, in effect, bring tangibles associated with the service to the forefront in communications strategy. For example, Carnival Cruise Lines' television advertising puts consumers "on the ship" by picturing vacationers dining, dancing, playing deck games, and, in general, having a wonderful time. The tangible of the cruise ship is presented as a destination rather than as transportation.

A second technique is to *create tangible representations of the service* to bolster communication of meaning and benefits. The Travelers Company's consistent, prominent use of a red umbrella in insurance advertising communicates the "protection" benefit of insurance while differentiating the company from competitors. McDonald's

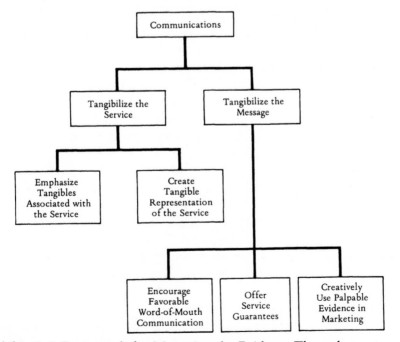

Exhibit 6–3 Framework for Managing the Evidence Through Communication

successful "Happy Meal" program for children illustrates the same technique of creating tangibles. By placing a burger and french fries into specially designed boxes festooned with games, mazes, and pictures of Ronald McDonald, McDonald's links entertainment and eating for a target market that is typically difficult for restaurants to please.

What the Carnival Cruise, Travelers, and McDonald's examples have in common is the use of tangibles to make the service itself seem more palpable and real. The examples differ because Carnival Cruise emphasizes a tangible inherent to the service, while Travelers and McDonald's create tangibles to represent the service. The latter examples differ further in that the red umbrella is strictly visual evidence, but the Happy Meal packaging is palpable to all senses.

Tangibilizing the Message. Marketers also may make the message about the service more tangible. One approach to tangibilizing the message is to *encourage favorable word-of-mouth communications.* When the consequences of selecting the *wrong* service supplier are high, the customer will be especially receptive to credible word-of-mouth communications from other customers to guide the decision-making process. This is why customers often seek the opinions of others before selecting a medical doctor, attorney, automobile mechanic, or college professor's class.

Smart marketers leverage the customer's propensity for receiving word-of-mouth communications in services. PHH Corporation (featured in the last chapter) actually pays the travel expenses of corporate prospects to visit satisfied PHH client firms to learn firsthand what those clients think of PHH. Many service companies feature the comments of satisfied customers in their advertising, effectively merging conventional and word-of-mouth advertising.[10]

Companies can also underscore the realness of their promises by *guaranteeing their services.* Long applied to goods marketing in the form of product warranties, the idea of guaranteeing services is newer. Its appeal seems to be growing rapidly, however, partly as the result of an excellent 1988 article on the subject, "The Power of Unconditional Service Guarantees."[11] The intended message of a service guarantee to customers is straightforward: "If our service were not excellent we could not possibly guarantee it." The message to employees may be even more powerful: "We must deliver excellent service because we are guaranteeing it."

When Bank One of Columbus, Ohio, acquired a failed Texas bank in 1989, it found itself in the unusual situation of having to start a trust company from scratch because the failed bank's trust department had been sold to a separate institution. Bank One hired a veteran Dallas trust banker—a crusty, no-nonsense, service-minded individual by the name of Richard Hart—to head up its new trust company in Texas. Hart then brought on board another Texas trust banker by the name of Garrett Jamison as senior vice president. Together they decided on an unconditional service quality guarantee as the linchpin of their marketing strategy. The guarantee is unconditional, simple to understand and communicate, meaningful, easy to invoke and collect on—the primary characteristics of an effective service guarantee.[12] It reads in full: "If you are not satisfied with our service quality in any given year, we will return to you the fees paid, or any portion thereof you feel is fair." The only other print on the page is one sentence naming who to contact within 90 days of the account year-end and giving a telephone number. That's it. No conditions except the 90-day reporting period. No strings. No exclusions. A very tangible message from the new kid on the block.

Still another approach to tangibilizing the message is the *creative use of palpable evidence in advertising*. In this case marketers consciously work to make the advertising message less abstract and more credible through the use of physical evidence. No service company is more clever at this than Southwest Airlines, one of America's most consistently profitable and lowest-fare airlines. In 1990 when Southwest launched its new Burbank–Oakland route, one of its advertising headlines stated: "Fly Southwest To Oakland and Get $127 Cash Back At The Gate." The body copy read, in part: "Just pay us the other airlines' ridiculously high regular coach fare of $186 from Burbank to Oakland, and we'll give you $127 cash back at the gate. Each way." When arch-rival America West ridiculed Southwest Airlines' no-frills approach to service by picturing actors in television advertising hiding their faces while boarding Southwest flights, Southwest responded with a television commercial featuring its chairman, Herb Kelleher, with a bag over his head. Kelleher's tangible message: "If you are embarrassed to fly Southwest, we will give you this bag to wear over your head. If you are not embarrassed, you can use the bag to keep all of the money you will save." At this point in the commercial, cash is dropped into the bag, filling it up.

PRICES

Marketing executives have a special interest in pricing because price is the only element of the marketing mix that generates revenue;

all other elements incur cost. However, price is important for another reason; customers use price as a clue about the product. Price can build up the customer's confidence in the product—or lessen it. Price can raise customer expectations ("this is expensive, it had better be good") or lower them ("you get what you pay for").

Setting the right price is especially important in services because of their intangibility. The invisibility of services makes that which is visible even more important to customers' purchasing decisions. Price is a visible indicator of a service's level and quality.

When Prices Are Too Low. Services marketers who set their prices too low potentially devalue their service to customers. Just how much expertise and skill support such a low-priced service, the customer wonders. Indeed, an interesting phenomenon in marketing is the tendency for companies with poor or mediocre quality reputations to use low price as a crutch to compensate for these deficiencies. This strategy usually fails because price and value are not the same thing. Value is the total benefit customers receive for the total "cost" they incur. Price is only one component of total cost. For example, a retailer with low prices, but also inattentive or incompetent service personnel and a messy, unclean store may actually be a "high-cost" retailer for many customers (and former customers).

As we write this book in 1990, the contrast between Southwest Airlines and Continental Airlines, two aggressive users of low fares as marketing tools, is revealing. Southwest is positioned as an efficient, reliable, no-frills, "fun" airline. Its on-time record is consistently high, and its reputation for safety is unparalleled in the U.S. airline industry. Launched as the "Luv" Airline, fun and zaniness permeate flight attendant service during the trip.

Southwest is able to offer low fares by foregoing certain customary services like interline baggage transfer, assigned seating, and food service. While it trades off these and other services, Southwest does not trade off the quality of the service it does offer. The net result is many fanatically loyal passengers who view the combination of consistent, everyday low fares *and* quality service as genuine value.

Continental Airlines, on the other hand, straddles the fence between a "full-service" airline and a discounter. It wants to charge full fares but frequently offers discounts because it cannot fill its seats otherwise. Once a proud trunk carrier, Continental went into a tailspin in 1983 when it filed for bankruptcy to abrogate its labor contracts and lower its labor costs. The resulting antagonism between management and labor diminished any real hope for improving service in the short term. And then in 1986 Texas Air (Continental's parent—now known as Continental Airlines Holdings Inc.) embarked on an acquisition binge by buying and trying to meld into the Continental system People Express and Frontier Airlines, two disparate and troubled airlines. In the same year, Texas Air also acquired Eastern Airlines, another seriously troubled carrier that ceased operations in 1991. Continental's service problems in the immediate aftermath of these acquisitions were significant, scaring away frequently flying business executives. The image problems persist.[13]

Here is our point: Whereas Southwest Airlines' pricing is appropriate to its strategic positioning, Continental's pricing is a reaction to its own difficulties. Southwest's low fares signal value to passengers who don't mind the lack of frills and tell those who do to stay away. Southwest's pricing offers clear and consistent evidence. On the other hand, Continental's heavy promotional activity spells out a confusing message for passengers. Is this an airline for executives or is this an airline for college kids and families flying on the cheap? Continental uses price as a crutch and the pricing evidence tells a muddled story.

When Prices Are Too High. Just as a price too low can send the wrong clues, so can a price too high. A price customers perceive as "too high" can convey an image of poor value, unconcern for customers, or "rip-off." America's automobile insurance industry is a case in point. Marketing a service that customers mostly think about when a premium statement arrives or when an accident occurs, auto insurers face an uphill public relations challenge even before they set their rates. Nevertheless, it is apparent that the majority of American drivers believe that auto insurance firms are charging excessive prices and they are angry about it.

In a 1990 national consumer poll conducted by Maritz Marketing Research, 63 percent of Americans indicated that they felt automobile insurance rates were too high. Alarmingly, 61 percent of the respondents indicated that the auto insurance industry needs more government regulation to guarantee fair practices and costs.[14]

Auto insurance executives might argue that the real culprits in high premium rates are an increasingly litigious society and lax drunk driving laws. But this is not the point we are making. The Maritz research clearly suggests that many policy holders *perceive* their insurance rates to be unfairly high. And it is perception that influences attitudes and behavior.

Prices send clues about the service just as the physical environment and communications do. A price can signal a "bare bones" service or a pampering service; it can signal a clear positioning strategy or a confused one; it can signal concern for the customer's welfare, or a lack of concern. Setting the right price in services is more than a matter of generating dollars today. It is also a matter of sending the right message about the service. Prices are evidence.

ROLES OF EVIDENCE

Having discussed the types of evidence to be managed (physical environment, communications, and prices), we now turn our attention to the *roles* of evidence. Clearly, the primary role for evidence management is to support the firm's marketing strategy. All other roles that we delineate in this section contribute to the overall role of supporting the marketing strategy. In developing a services marketing strategy, marketers should consider specifically how the manipulation of tangibles can provide customers and employees a mental picture of the strategy, and how they want customers and employees to feel and respond.[15]

The idea of managing evidence for employees as well as for customers may seem unusual. We feel strongly about it, however. Service personnel not only sell and deliver services to customers—they *are* the service to many customers. Ensuring that employees *understand* and *buy into* the service and its strategy is critical. Service employees need a mental picture of the invisible service, too. (We develop this point later in this section and consider the broader topic of employees as customers in Chapter 9).

Tangibles can underscore or undermine the overall services marketing strategy. Consider, for example, the case of Qantas Airlines, the Australian national airline, and how its consistent use in advertising of the koala bear underscores its positioning as the airline that flies to and knows Australia. On the other hand, reflect on how much of the tangible evidence in many of America's shopping malls undermines the strategy of attracting older customers who have the most spending power. As consultant Francesca Turchiano writes:

> The intangible qualities sought by older adults are not easily found in a shopping center environment. . . . Rest rooms are often difficult to find; mall seating is often sparse to deter teens

from loitering; mall directories are often out of date and printed in small type; and salespeople are often underpaid, undertrained, unfriendly, and impersonal. A tenant mix that is often weighted toward apparel and other merchandise aimed at younger women doesn't help either.[16]

Various subroles potentially contribute to the marketing strategy support role of evidence management. Marketers can use evidence for some or all of these subroles as conditions dictate. Not mutually exclusive, these subroles for evidence include:

- Shaping first impressions
- Managing trust
- Facilitating quality service
- Changing an image
- Providing sensory stimulation
- Socializing employees

As shown pictorially in Exhibit 6–4, to be effective, these roles should be consistent with and reinforce a company's marketing strategy.

SHAPING FIRST IMPRESSIONS

Tangibles can play a disproportionately important role in influencing customers who have little or no other experience with a firm. In the absence of other information about a service, customers rely heavily on visible clues. This is what Professor Jean-Charles Chebat of the Université du Quebec à Montreal means when he states, "The more expert the customer, the less sensitive he or she is to the tangible dimensions." Professor Mary Jo Bitner of Arizona State University uses the example of a lawyer's office furniture, decor, and clothing influencing a prospective client's beliefs about whether the lawyer is successful or not successful, expensive or not expensive, and trustworthy or not trustworthy.[17]

Coldwell Banker, the prominent real estate company, arms its residential sales associates with a variety of tangible materials they can use to sign up clients. The components of Coldwell Banker's "Best Seller System" (the firm also has a "Best Buyer System") include:

- *Best Seller Listing Presentation Guide*—a publication that answers the most frequently asked questions by sellers when selecting a real estate company

Exhibit 6–4 Relationships Between Roles of Evidence and Marketing Strategy

- *Best Seller Action Plan*—a marketing plan tailored for the specific property
- *Best Seller Marketing Services Guarantee*—promised actions for marketing the property guaranteed in writing
- *Best Seller Home Enhancement Guide*—a publication with home enhancement ideas and work sheets.

Collectively, these materials help sales agents foster a client prospect's first impression of competence, commitment, and personalized service. The tangibles reinforce the verbal promises. Jack Hull, retired national marketing director for Coldwell Banker Residential Sales states: "There is little of tangible substance in helping people buy and sell a home. We developed the Best Buyer and Seller Systems to provide our sales associates with ways to tangibilize what they do when working with buyers and sellers. The Systems go a long way in taking the mystery out of the transaction for the customer."

MANAGING TRUST

Coldwell Banker's Best Buyer and Best Seller Systems are useful in shaping first impressions because they convey trust. The company uses tangible materials to teach the client what to do and to back up what it will do. Effective services marketing depends on the management of trust because the customer typically must buy a service before fully experiencing it. As PHH Corporation's Gene Arbaugh puts it, "The most difficult aspect of marketing a service is the fact that you are selling a number of promises to be delivered sometime in the future."

P. Anne van't Haaff, Head of Corporate Quality at KLM Royal Dutch Airlines, emphasizes the need to manage trust for what he labels "black box" services. He states:

We as individuals cannot possibly know how the systems work. We have to trust the reliability of our computers, cars, or aircraft. We expect to arrive on time together with our baggage. We expect light when we flip a switch. We can only trust that our expectations are met, because as individual customers or users we have no influence on the process. We often cannot help ourselves when something goes wrong. The black box society is based on trust.[18]

Professor Evert Gummesson of the Service Research Center at the University of Karlstad in Sweden suggests moving the line of visibility for the service to show the customer what really goes on to deliver it. Lexus allows the customer "backstage" by designing its automobile dealership facilities to include a large window that permits customers to look into the service bays. The window conveys to customers that the company is proud of the work its service technicians do.[19]

Benihana of Tokyo, the restaurant chain, achieves a similar result by transforming the traditionally hidden food preparation service into a theatrical "frontstage" performance. At Benihana the chef comes right up to the hibachi table where diners sit, bows, sets down the uncooked food, asks diners how they want their meals prepared, with dramatic flair and rhythm cuts the food into bite-size morsels, and cooks the meal with all the sizzle possible.

Coldwell Banker, Lexus, and Benihana of Tokyo are using tangibles to reveal more of the service. They are attempting to earn the customers' confidence by being more open and forthcoming than competitors about the service. In effect, they are managing the customers' trust by opening Anne van't Haaff's "black box."

FACILITATING QUALITY SERVICE

The management of tangibles also plays a role in customers' service quality perceptions. As we discussed earlier in the book, tangibles are a "process" dimension of service—i.e., customers make judgments about the quality of tangibles *during* the service process. Through tangibles associated with the service experience, marketers have the opportunity to reinforce other service quality dimensions with a quality look. By "quality look" we do not mean necessarily "expensive" or "elegant." What we do mean is attention to basics such as cleanliness, orderliness, and customer-friendly systems. We also mean the use of evidence appropriate to the target market and overall marketing strategy.

Professor Mary Jo Bitner, in an experimental study, showed travelers a booklet that described a scenario in which an airline passenger requests from a travel agency the lowest possible airfare between two cities. During the flight, the passenger learns that another person on board paid a lower fare. Two versions of the booklet describing this scenario were prepared. They were identical except for a photograph featuring the travel agent at her desk. One photograph showed the agent in a neat, organized office setting. In the other booklet, the photograph showed the agent in a disorganized office setting. Respondents exposed to the booklet picturing the disorganized service environment were more likely to attribute responsibility for the deficient service to the travel agency and more likely to expect the same type of problem to occur in the future.[20]

One marketer who successfully manages the tangibles to facilitate quality service is Manhattan pediatrician, Laura Popper. Dr. Popper's waiting room walls are bright white trimmed with strawberry-red paint. She herself forgoes the traditional doctor's white coat for colorful clothing and always wears slacks because "they are great for crawling all over the floor with the kids." Dr. Popper states, "In starting my practice, I thought very much about my office, and that I wanted patients to be comfortable and happy here. I wanted it to represent what I am and what I hope to give people. My consultation room is all toys. Kids cry when they have to leave the office."

Improving quality through tangibles means attention to the smallest detail that competitors might consider trivial and unworthy of investment. Yet, it is the visible details that can add up for customers and signal a stronger message of caring and competence. Russell Vernon, president of West Point Market, a highly acclaimed food store in Akron, Ohio, garnishes his food display cases with fresh flowers. Robert Onstead, founding partner and chairman of Randall's Food and Drugs, a 40-plus store supermarket chain in Houston, insists on angled parking spaces in front of his stores because they are easier for customers. Onstead also lights his parking lots with candlepower well above code so that customers can feel more secure visiting his stores after dark. Disney doesn't sell gum in its theme parks because the sight of gum stuck to the pavement isn't what a fantasy land is supposed to look like.

CHANGING AN IMAGE

The management of evidence is a primary tool for service firms seeking an image change. Changing an image is challenging because it involves breaking down existing attitudes, not just adding something new. Service intangibility increases the challenge. Without a tangible product to be the central carrier of newly intended messages, services marketers must find other tangibles to serve as surrogate media. Spoken words alone usually will not be sufficient to persuade an organization's public that the organization is no longer "Y" but is now "X." The message of change must be visual, too.

Consider the case of the Girl Scouts of the U.S.A., an organization in the 1970s that was not compatible with the growing cultural diversity and career-mindedness of young girls in America. In 1970, Girl Scouts of the U.S.A. had 3.9 million members; by 1976 when Frances Hesselbein became National Executive Director of the organization, membership had fallen to 3.16 million. Hesselbein's goals were to change the service to fit the market and to make sure the market was aware the service was changing. The management of evidence was a key tool. Under Hesselbein's leadership, the organization recruited fashion designers Bill Blass and Halston to update the adult uniform line, emphasized finding successful women role models in business and other professions to serve as troop leaders and volunteers, and published handbook materials in additional languages.[21]

Frances Hesselbein used visual symbolism to help change the image of the Girl Scouts. She tangibilized her vision of the new Girl Scouts of the U.S.A. and didn't rely on words alone. Her efforts have paid off in a stabilized base of slightly more than three million members in the early 1990s, following the precipitous membership decline in the 1970s.

PROVIDING SENSORY STIMULATION

Still another potential subrole for evidence is to give the marketing strategy an entertainment edge. Services marketers who use evidence to entertain seek to inject novelty, excitement, and fun into the customer's consumption experience. These marketers trade on the unusual; they challenge customer boredom head-on; they view the service setting as a stage and service delivery as theatre.

Disney's newer Orlando hotels, the Walt Disney World Swan Hotel (with a pair of 28-ton swan sculptures on its roof) and its companion, the Walt Disney World Dolphin (crowned with concrete dolphins), illustrate what the company refers to as "entertainment architecture." Designed by post-modernist architect, Michael Graves, the hotels extend the perception of fantasy from the company's theme parks; they make the Disney experience richer and fuller than if visitors were to sleep in a clean and modern, but nondescript, hotel. Replete with creative flourishes and visual mischief (the Swan Hotel has two-dimensional potted palms in its lobby, for example), the two hotels are connected by a tented walkway over a lake. They are but the first of a series of signature buildings that Disney has commissioned well-known architects to design.[22]

Architecture can be a valuable source of evidentiary support for a sensory-based marketing strategy, but it is not the only—or necessarily the most compelling—source of this support. Architecture is the outer wrapping of the package, an initial set of clues. It is critical that the interior wrappings—the ambience, the customer systems, the employees' appearance and attitudes—build on the initial message or that message becomes a lie.

Stew Leonard's, the famous food store that does $3,400 a square foot in sales in its flagship Norwalk, Connecticut store, is a company whose magic is mostly inside the building. The Stew Leonard family loves its customers and this attitude permeates the interior building, making it come alive in a sensory collage of sights, sounds, and smells.

At Stew Leonard's the evidence of customer love is everywhere: cartoon characters roam the store aisles shaking hands with customers, posing for pictures, and handing out free food samples; in-store robots serenade customers walking by with their shopping carts; a mechanical cow moos whenever a little kid (or a big kid) presses its nose (which happens 1,000 times a day); a policy of over-staffing checkout lines ("We would rather wait than have our customers wait," states Stew Leonard, Jr., the president); a big light at each checkout stand that flashes whenever a customer spends more than $100—earning the customer a free pint of ice cream. What all of this—and more—adds up to is what Stew Leonard, Jr. calls the "WOW" factor. He states:

> The "WOW" factor is trying to create a retail environment where the customer actually says "WOW!" The "WOW factor" is an attempt to make the shopping experience fun for the customer. We'll have a live band come and play in the store on holidays. Lots of samples, even real friendly people make the customer say "WOW!"
>
> We had a customer come in and say he bought $34 worth of fresh lobsters, but had to throw them out because the shell was too thick and he couldn't eat them. He was instantly given his $34 back in cash. He said, "WOW! You don't get treated like that in other food stores!" Only happy customers come back. Many consumers look at food shopping as a drudgery. Our goal is to get them to have fun, bring their kids to the animal farm and make the trip a family outing.

SOCIALIZING EMPLOYEES

Services are intangible for employees just as they are for customers. One way to support the marketing strategy through evidence is to make sure the evidence conveys the right mental picture of the service to the employees carrying out the strategy. This is partly what Disney chairman and CEO Michael Eisner has in mind with his aggressive use of architecture as a marketing tool. Speaking of his new Orlando hotels and others to come, Eisner states: "Our own people have to be educated. Our own people have to say, every time they do something, 'Am I doing it with style? Am I doing it with taste?'"[23]

By managing tangibles, marketers have an opportunity to teach employees more about the service and its benefits, guide employees' behavior in performing the service, and convey concern for the welfare and comfort of employees. By providing its sales agents with a tangible system for preparing a customized property marketing plan,

Coldwell Banker increases the probability that its agents will actually prepare such a plan. By publishing home enhancement ideas for clients, Coldwell Banker teaches these same ideas to the sales agents. Stew Leonard's in-store mechanical cow, singing robots, and cartoon characters create an upbeat atmosphere for employees as well as for customers. The unconditional service guarantee Bank One Texas offers its trust company clients is a constant reminder to its own personnel to return client calls promptly, prepare well for client visits, and proofread all documentation.

With our former student, Julie Baker, we have studied empirically customer and employee reaction to branch banking facilities. We found that bank employees rate the overall importance of the branch environment significantly higher than do bank customers. Although both groups place the physical environment above the midpoint on a seven-point scale, it is not surprising that employees rate it higher given that they spend more of their time in the service facility than do customers.[24]

Our research suggests that the tangibles in the work environment symbolize to employees management's level of concern for them. Even the most enlightened executive can overlook the negative impact of unmanaged evidence on employees, as the following story from Carl Sewell's book attests:

> We used to have a locker room for our technicians that was pretty awful, and I will never forget being at a dinner for our technicians and having our front-end tech, Sam McFarland, come over to me and say, "Carl, you may take care of your customers, but sometimes you forget about your employees. Have you looked at our rest rooms? *Do you think we live like that at home?*" Well, that was humbling. A week later we had a carpenter crew in there, and we tore it out and rebuilt it and did it right.[25]

SUMMARY AND ACTION CHECKLIST

One key to successful services marketing is managing the tangibles associated with the intangible service to help customers better understand what they are buying and why they should buy it. With no "tires to kick" in advance of a service purchase, customers look for surrogate evidence in the service environment, communications, and prices to guide their choice. The more important and riskier the purchase, the more likely it is that customers will search for and process the available evidence, both positive and negative.

Smart services marketers manage the evidence to send the right clues. They realize that customers ". . . like detectives [will] deduce the quality, the value and the nature of the service by judging the tangible clues."[26] The question is whether these customers will judge managed or unmanaged clues.

The primary role of evidence management is to support the marketing strategy. The clever use of tangibles can give customers and employees a vivid picture of the service and its positioning despite the service's intangible core. The subroles of evidence we discussed in this chapter have in common the potential to support the marketing strategy: shaping first impressions, managing trust, facilitating quality service, changing an image, providing sensory stimulation, and socializing employees.

Effectively managing service evidence is more than tactics, more than strategy. Primarily, it is an attitude of giving shape and substance to a service that otherwise would be difficult to comprehend. It is an attitude of innovating, of exceeding the norm, to create a special perception of the service on the part of customers and employees. It is an attitude of caring about the details of the business, the 101 "little things" that add up and make a difference. The best "evidence" we can give you that managing the evidence is more attitude than anything else is to present Exhibit 6–5, written by Russell Vernon, the president of one of America's most successful specialty food stores, the West Point Market in Akron, Ohio.

ACTION CHECKLIST

Managing the evidence is *not* just the marketing department's job. The marketing department should set the tone, but everyone has a responsibility to help send the right clues about the service. Here is an "action checklist" of questions that *all* managers in the organization should ask regularly:

1. *Do we take a holistic approach to evidence management in this company?* Are we sufficiently mindful that everything customers can sense about the service is evidence?

2. *Are we proactive in managing evidence?* Do we actively discuss how we can use tangibles to strengthen our service concept, to strengthen our message?

Exhibit 6–5 Managing the Evidence at the West Point Market

Managing the tangibles associated with a service begins with becoming directly involved and having a commitment from the top. It is not cheap, easy or quick, but an ongoing, day-to-day attitude that permeates the company and bonds staff member to staff member and applies total company resources to customer satisfaction.

Managing the tangibles means as president of the West Point Market I work the sales floor helping shoppers, packing and carrying out groceries. Top management's attitude toward service tells all staff people how important the customer is. This is leadership by example, top down.

It means your trucks are clean and in excellent mechanical condition so that deliveries are made on time and the truck reflects the high quality of products and services offered by your company.

It means Monday morning breakfasts with three staff members each week where we discuss my business philosophy on the care and handling of our customers. With 111 associates this takes almost one year to complete. When they leave the breakfast table all understand customer service from my personal experience and point of view and how critical this is to the success of our company.

It means miniature shopping carts "for our little shoppers only" along with our "cookie credit" from the bakery and balloons for the kids.

It means our restrooms feature fresh flowers, turn of the century art, indirect lighting, classical music and Swedish Almond soap. That is tangible evidence that I care that the customer came to the West Point Market.

It means that our service clerks who carry groceries out have with them umbrellas for our customers during rainy periods and snow scrapers to clean windows in the winter months.

It means a licensed dietician on hand Saturdays for our customers so that they might have answers to nutrition questions and discuss health issues and food values.

Finally, to manage the evidence we have orchestrated our retail sales floor to function as an event. Our customers can expect new sounds, new looks, new feelings, new excitement, new tastes and new smells when they shop with us. It is the drum and bagpipe corps, double decker bus rides, a big, walking, talking chicken near our fresh eggs . . . it's 200 American flags on the property . . . it's thousands of plants, flowers and 80 trees surrounding the store. It is show business, and it drives our company.

By Russell B. Vernon, President.

3. *Do we manage the details well?* Do we worry about the "little things"? Do we insist on spotless service facilities, for example? When a bulb burns out in one of our electric signs, do we change it immediately or eventually? Do we, as managers, teach our people by the example we set that no detail is too small to manage?

4. *Do we incorporate evidence management into our marketing planning?* Do we consider facilities design decisions, for example, to be marketing decisions in support of the marketing strategy? Do we, as managers, know the roles of evidence in

our marketing plan so that we can help implement the plan? Do we, as managers, know what is in the marketing plan at all?

5. *Do we use research to guide our evidence-management decisions?* Do we seek input from customers and employees about the clues our prices send? Do we pretest our advertising with customers and employees to learn what clues the advertising is transmitting? Do we seek the input of customers and employees *during* the design of our service facilities? Do we hire professional "shoppers" to visit our facilities and rate them on criteria such as cleanliness, neatness, and the proper use of marketing materials? Do we, as managers, "shop" our facilities and review our other forms of evidence within the context of improving our overall message?

6. *Do we spread ownership of evidence management throughout the organization?* Do we teach our people about the nature and importance of evidence management in service businesses? Do we ask everyone in our organization to assume personal responsibility for managing the evidence?

7. *Are we innovative in our evidence management?* Do we do anything differently from our competitors and other service providers? Is there any originality in what we do? Do we regularly update and otherwise improve our evidence or do we lapse into complacency?

8. *Do we manage first impressions well?* Are we impressive or mediocre in the early moments of a customer's experience with us? Do our advertisements, our exterior and interior facilities, our signage, and our employees' attitudes captivate or annoy new customers and customer prospects?

9. *Do we invest in our employees' appearance?* Do we distribute clothing and personal grooming guidelines to our employees if appropriate to their work role? Have we considered uniforms or clothing allowances for customer-contact employees? Have we considered offering personal grooming classes?

10. *Do we manage evidence for our employees?* Do we use tangibles to help demystify the service for employees, and to them in performing their service role? Do the tangibles work environment convey management's concern for ees, or lack of concern?

7

◇◇◇

Branding the Company

In this chapter, we turn our attention to managing a special form of evidence: the service brand. Although branding is most identified with packaged goods marketing, it is a critical issue in services marketing as well.

The essential purpose of a brand is to distinguish one company's offerings from that of other companies. Consisting of names and other distinguishing elements such as slogans and symbols, brands provide customers an efficient mechanism for identifying a particular firm or its products. Achieving distinction from competitors is no less important for firms marketing services than for firms marketing goods.

In services marketing the company brand is the primary brand; in packaged goods marketing the product brand is the primary brand. The locus of brand impact is different for packaged goods and services because services lack the inherent physical presence that facilitates individual product packaging, labeling, and display. Even the most clever evidence manager will find it difficult to affix a brand on a service-product like electricity. Thus, in services, the company brand becomes paramount. Customers buying Prell, Comet, Pampers, or Charmin may not know or care that the maker is Procter & Gamble. But with services, customers select or reject the company brand—Avis, H&R Block, Federal Express.

The locus of brand impact shifts from product brand to company brand as service plays a greater role in determining a product's value to customers. Thus, the company brand name of Procter & Gamble, while playing a secondary role with consumers, significantly influences wholesale and retail distributors because these resellers rely ore heavily on Procter & Gamble's service. For the same reason, company branding is critically important for industrial goods manufacturers like IBM, Corning, and Dow Chemical.

A MODEL OF SERVICES BRANDING

The principal elements and influences in services branding are shown in Exhibit 7–1. A service company presents its brand to customers, customer-prospects, employees, and other stakeholders

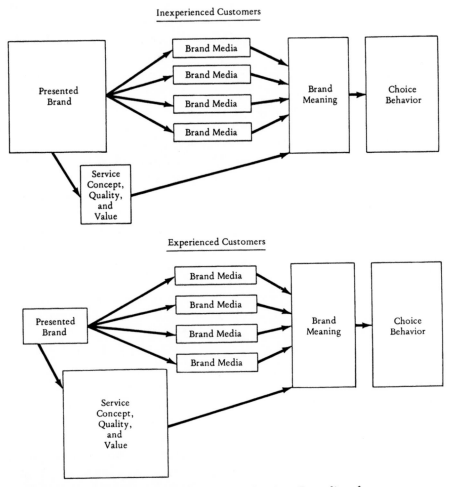

Exhibit 7–1 Elements and Influences in Services Branding for Inexperienced and Experienced Customers

through a variety of potential media, including facilities, signs, print and television advertising, delivery trucks, employee uniforms, and more. The core of the presented brand is the company's name, but the accompanying words and symbols, and the visual presentation of these stimuli, play key roles also.

The brand the company presents is not necessarily the brand the customer perceives, however. The construct, *brand meaning*, is the customer's snapshot impression *and* classification of the firm. As alluded to in the last chapter, the meaning of the brands Southwest Airlines and Continental Airlines for individual travelers extends beyond the literal names and influences their preference. To one traveler, Southwest Airlines may mean value and dependability. To another, the brand may mean no food, no preassigned seats, no frills.

Brand meaning is a function of brand presentation *and* service concept, quality, and value. The service the company provides, how well it performs the service, and the service's value combine to influence customers' interpretations of the presented brand. Managers cannot erect walls around the company brand to shield it from customers' actual experiences with the company; what managers can do is create a service that reinforces the intended brand image.

Customers' experience-based beliefs are powerful, diminishing the effects of company-controlled communications that contradict actual experience. This is why the service concept, quality, and value box in Exhibit 7–1 is larger than the presented brand box for *experienced customers*. An excellent branding strategy can make a strong service stronger, but it cannot rescue a weak service. Although strong branding can help draw new customers to the firm, it does not compensate for a weak service the customer experiences. What does the firm do for its second act when the actual service doesn't live up to its advance billing? Customers' negative experience with the service can close the doors that branding helps to open.

Branding is a tool—a form of evidence—that helps the best-managed service companies the most. Its principal role is to give the firm a *marketing* edge by reinforcing the firm's service in a way that is differentiating, important, and commanding to customers. We asked several executives to tell us which American service company has the strongest brand identity and why. Their answers appear in Exhibit 7–2. Note how each answer reveals the influence of a strong service on brand meaning and the marketing edge the strong brand gives the company.

An effective brand provides a marketing edge to service companies under a variety of conditions, including:

Exhibit 7-2 Which Service Company Has the Strongest Brand Identity: Three Opinions

I can't help but think of Federal Express. They have done an excellent job of convincing me — through their performance — that they can deliver what they promise at a reasonable price . . . and what they promise is a service that I need in my business. Their name is consistent with their mission and the focus of their organization. I think their business service strengths would translate well into the passenger airline business where I would love to see them compete. That is possibly the strongest endorsement for them.

— Abbey R. Chung, Director
Corporate Quality Improvement
Johnson & Johnson Medical, Inc.

The golden arches and Mc-whatever identify fast food, fun and value for the dollar spent. In my travels around the Virginia-Maryland area, I know exactly what to expect when I see the golden arches and McDonalds' ability to be "reliable" is superb. Furthermore, the strength of the brand is reinforced by McDonalds' success in Europe and in other countries.

The brand "McDonalds" is so strong that it becomes the standard of comparison. I work closely with a family restaurant franchise in this area, and a constant standard of comparison is McDonalds. Whatever McDonalds tries, however it innovates, its competitors must monitor because McDonalds establishes the standard by which all will be judged.

— Alexander B. Berry, III
Senior Executive Vice President
Signet Bank

Cable News Network (CNN) is viewed throughout the world as one of the most respected and relied upon sources of accurate news information. In the "information age," CNN represents the way many get accurate information. It has proven to be a way for Americans to get accurate facts about current events occurring in our country and throughout the world. It is also the way that many other countries have been able to see what democracy has to offer. Due to their timely and accurate dissemination of news, it is probably accurate to state that CNN can take some of the credit for the exciting changes that are happening currently in our world.

— Thomas F. Gillett, Vice President
Business Development and
Technology Transfer
Cable Television Laboratories, Inc.

- When customers perceive competitors to be similar in service concept, quality, and value
- When customers have little or no experience with competing firms and respond to the strongest presented brand
- When a firm wishes to enter a related service category and extends its brand to the new category

- When a firm launches an innovative new service
- When a firm changes its marketing strategy and uses a new branding strategy to help communicate the new direction

Strong service brands help customers to visualize, understand, and believe in the service. They reduce customers' perceived monetary, social, or safety risk in buying services that are difficult to evaluate prior to purchase. They reassure customers purchasing the "black box" services we referred to in the last chapter. In research conducted in England, Professor Chris Easingwood studied the factors that inhibit effective competitive response to successful service innovations. Easingwood identified ten factors that made it more difficult for firms to respond effectively to a competitor's innovation. The two most important factors: company reputation and branding.[1]

NAMES—THE CORE OF SERVICE BRANDS

Having noted the influence of the service on brand meaning, we now turn our attention to the presented brand, the focus of this chapter. The company name is the core element of the presented brand. Although it is possible to build an effective service brand from a weak name, it is clearly easier to do so when the name is strong.

We propose four tests for assessing the brand power of a name:[2]

1. *Distinctiveness.* The name immediately distinguishes the firm from competitors.
2. *Relevance.* The name conveys the nature or benefit of the service.
3. *Memorability.* The name can be understood, used, and recalled easily.
4. *Flexibility.* The name accommodates the inevitable strategy changes in organizations.

DISTINCTIVENESS

A distinctive service brand is more difficult to establish with a name based on frequently used generic terms. Words like National, United, and Allied are too familiar and too broadly used to meet the distinctiveness test. National what? Which United? Allied who?

More words are needed—Car Rental, Airlines, Stores—just to identify the company's line of business.

In financial services marketing, bank names based on words like "First," "Commerce," "National," or "Merchants" have lost their cachet as competitors have proliferated and marketing boundaries have expanded. As recently as 1983, four of the largest banks in the state of Virginia were Virginia National Bank, First Virginia Bank, Bank of Virginia and United Virginia Bank. All have since changed their names, but previously the names of these competitors blurred together unnecessarily. No wonder financial institutions have been changing their names at a more feverish pace than any other type of service provider in recent years.

One way to achieve name distinctiveness is to use words that are uncommon to the service category. Meridian and Fleet are distinctive bank names because they are uncommon within financial services. Proper names, such as family names, also can stand out in a crowded communications environment. Consider how powerful names such as J. P. Morgan, McDonald's, and Marriott have become. A third alternative, fabricated words, is becoming more prevalent as proper nouns and real words become less available. Unfortunately, some of these fabrications are too extreme, too obviously the product of a computer. Names like Allegis and Synovus suggest images of far-off galaxies rather than excellent service companies. In these instances, however, the problem lies in the execution of the approach and not in the approach itself. For example, a fabricated name such as Citibank certainly serves its purpose well.

RELEVANCE

A name that communicates the nature or benefit of a service helps to identify and position a company in customers' minds. Ticketron suggests both the nature of the service and its electronic delivery. Visa implies international access, a useful message for a brand name under which credit card services are marketed and used worldwide. Humana connotes caring, sensitive service—especially positive connotations for a health-care company.

One of the most relevant service brand names we have discovered is Bank of Granite—a name that dates back to 1906 when the bank was founded in Granite Falls, North Carolina. The bank's chairman and chief executive, John Forlines, Jr. comments:

I just can't tell you how pleased we are with the name, particularly during the period that banking's been going through for
the last number of years. . . . We feel like this gives us
something to hang our hat on, something to work real hard for
to be sure that we are as solid as the name implies.[3]

Incidentally, Bank of Granite thus far is doing a good job living up
to its name. As of 1990, the $300 million bank had increased cash
dividends to shareholders for 36 years straight.

Relevance does not mean description. A name that literally describes the service usually is disadvantageous because description can
increase length and decrease distinctiveness. Overnight Mail Services, for example, would be relevant, but is a weaker name than
Federal Express. Personal Touch Health Care is weaker than Humana. Names that resonate with indirect connotations, rather than
literal descriptions, also are more likely to meet the third test, memorability.

MEMORABILITY

Several factors can contribute to a memorable brand name. Distinctiveness is one. Sovran is more memorable than First Union, Bell-
South more memorable than US West. But a name that is distinctive
because it is complex or based on difficult words may flunk the memorability test.

Brevity and simplicity are generally assets in a brand name. Easy
pronunciation encourages memorability. Travelers is more user-
friendly than Massachusetts Mutual Life, for example.

Brevity and simplicity also facilitate effective graphic treatment in
a logo. Indeed, firms with long names often are forced to abbreviate
them to fit the requirements of visual presentation. Whether the
shortened form is selected by the company or its customers, the result
is that the service entity has two names—Great Atlantic & Pacific
Tea and A&P, Consolidated Edison of New York and Con Ed. In
cases such as A&P and Con Ed, double names do not pose a problem. In other cases, long or difficult names are problematic, for example the unflattering nickname "Monkey Ward" for Montgomery
Ward.

When it is done with restraint and dignity, an unusual spelling can
aid memorability. Toys R Us increases memorability by using the
single letter instead of the word "are" and by reversing the "R" in the
presented brand.

FLEXIBILITY

Because change in the nature and scope of the service offering is inevitable, an effective service branding program should accommodate this natural process. A long time horizon, preferably twenty years or more, should be used in assessing how a service organization might outgrow its current—or contemplated—name.

Geographic designations are one trap to avoid. When airlines responded to deregulation by developing new route structures, many found their name to be restrictive and inappropriate for the broader marketing areas. USAir was adopted in 1979 to replace the regionalism of Allegheny when the company became a full-scale domestic carrier. And even the USAir name does not accommodate route expansion outside the United States. Western Hotels became Western International (a confusing identity) and changed again to Westin, a fabricated name with less of a regional connotation.

Any descriptively limiting term can inhibit the perception that a company's scope of activities has changed. A firm that has evolved into a total transportation company is less likely to have its broader scope of services be fully appreciated with a word like "trucking" or "rail" in its name. An even more serious problem arises if the name restricts *internal* comprehension of the company's potential, verbally painting management's own perception into a corner.

Connotations usually are more flexible than denotations. Sentry can evolve better than Insurance Company of North America. Even the use of the initials, INA, does not solve the inflexibility problem completely. It takes many years to establish the kind of recognition enjoyed by IBM and AT&T. In the meantime, customers may ask, "What does INA stand for?" and the company remains stuck in a descriptive straightjacket.

BRANDS ARE MORE THAN NAMES

The presented brand is a total concept based on far more than a name alone. Its effectiveness depends on the integration of words, colors, symbols, and slogans, and the consistent application of these elements across all brand media. The effective blending of all communication elements into a cohesive image, and fidelity in their use, are a powerful antidote to the intangible, amorphous nature of services.

Lynn Newman, who heads the Minneapolis office of Maritz Marketing Research, makes the case well for cohesiveness and consistency in services branding:

> One of the most important steps a service marketer can take in creating a strong brand identity is to develop a consistent presentation of the visible elements of the service. By visible elements I mean the company's name, logo, colors, uniforms, and equipment. The more consistent a company's "appearance" is to consumers, the stronger the brand identity. This is especially true for service companies with multiple locations such as banks, hotels, and restaurants. Examples of companies with consistent visible elements include Pizza Hut—the red roof, and McDonalds—the golden arches.
>
> An example of a company with inconsistent visible elements is Northwest Airlines. Many years ago it dropped "Orient" from its name, yet the name Northwest Orient still appears in signage at some airport locations. The airline's management recognizes that the company does not have a consistent, coherent image and it is currently changing many of the visible elements—a new logo, new paint design for aircraft, new signage. This is an expensive, time-consuming endeavor but the quicker it is completed the better. Airline passengers cannot be expected to have a strong brand identity with an airline that is known by two different names, that has two different logos, and that has aircraft with a variety of colors and designs.

Some brands that are less than optimal on the basis of four tests have become powerful anyway due to coordinated, consistent presentation and strong service performance. ARA is hardly a terrific name and yet the company clearly commands a marketing edge from this brand. Formerly doing business under more than 50 different logos and 250 different names, today ARA does business under one easy-to-read logo and just 25 division names, all clearly connected to the parent company name. The firm has turned its fleet of more than 20,000 trucks into "rolling billboards" for the ARA brand and has put all of its service employees in ARA uniforms. ARA boosted its brand further through its highly visible involvement as the official supplier of food and transportation services to the 1984 Summer and Winter Olympics.[4]

Graphic symbols can help make a fair name better and a good name great. Consider the role that symbolism plays in the branding of Prudential of America. The Prudential name has distinctiveness, relevance, memorability, and flexibility. Yet, it has been the disciplined association of this name with the Rock of Gibraltar symbol (both as originally drawn and the more recent abstract version) that transformed a strong verbal element into an even stronger verbal-visual unit. The Prudential "Rock" is ever present, anchoring and announcing the brand simultaneously.

Slogans can also add power to a brand name. "You're in good hands with Allstate" conveys with words and the visual image of the insurance agent's cupped hands what policyholders can expect from the company. "Fly the friendly skies of United" distinguishes and makes relevant a bland name.

Maximizing the effectiveness and efficiency of the presented brand requires the *creativity* to tell a meaningful story through a variety of verbal-visual elements and the *discipline* to tell only one story. We now turn to a discussion of guidelines for implementing a strong branding effort.

GUIDELINES FOR BUILDING A BRAND

Although we have focused on branding in this chapter, we have already planted most of the seeds for this subject in earlier chapters. In the first chapters we stressed that service quality is the foundation for services marketing; in the present chapter, we illustrate this point by showing the interplay between company-controlled branding and service performance in creating *brand meaning*.

In Chapter 5, we discussed image management as one of three primary roles for service firm marketing directors. And in Chapter 6 we introduced the concept of evidence management, of which company branding is a part.

At this stage of the book, then, the reader will not be surprised by our positioning of branding as a central, strategic marketing tool for service firms. What are some of the guidelines marketers should bear in mind as they seek to build a powerful company brand? We offer the following:

- Start with research
- Select the right medicine
- Build on what exists
- Internalize the brand

START WITH RESEARCH

Brand development relies heavily on research, for research findings clarify what needs to be done. Building a brand involves brand-building decisions and the issue is whether these decisions are to be based on research data or made without them.

Among the important, researchable questions in formulating branding strategy are:

- What is the company's current brand meaning to customers and others (including managers, other employees, and former customers)?
- How does the company's brand meaning compare with that of key competitors?
- How well does the company name meet the tests of a good name?
- How well do brand elements other than the names perform their roles compared to key competitors?
- What are the relative effects of service concept, quality, and value on brand meaning for the company and its competitors?
- What is important about the company's service offering that could be conveyed by the brand?

In brief, services marketers want to build a company brand that expresses the firm's strongest qualities, its "reason for being," in a compelling way for customers, prospects, and other stakeholders. Good information will help marketers meet this objective. Edwin Lefkowith, president of Lefkowith Inc., a corporate communications company in New York City, underscores the role of research in the following comment:

> To be properly focused in branding, you must understand what unique qualities best characterize and differentiate your company and its services among your satisfied customers. You must carve out a niche that is both appropriate and advantageous for your company.

Branding research normally should take several forms, ranging from executive interviews and customer focus group interviews to industry-wide brand meaning surveys. In addition, observational research is necessary to monitor the consistency and fidelity of brand presentation across media, specific services, and markets. Moreover, because brand meaning is a function of dynamic influences, and thus is itself a dynamic construct, branding research must be performed on an ongoing basis. Services marketers need to install an ongoing brand research process, not just conduct a branding study.

SELECT THE RIGHT MEDICINE

One of the temptations to guard against in company branding is to ask more of this tool than it can possibly deliver. As we have already stressed, a poor service offering cannot be overcome with excellent branding techniques. Just as a shiny new package won't compensate for an inferior product inside, neither will a new corporate name or fancy new logo overcome a flawed service concept or mediocre quality.

Nonetheless, it is tempting to expect miracles from a new branding strategy. Change the operating name. Brighten the color scheme. Modernize the logo. Double the advertising budget. And the patient will be cured.

In reality, of course, the patient remains ill. Our advice is: continually work to improve the whole service-product—the performance, not just the "package." Implement a branding strategy to communicate a strong service offering, not as a substitute for a strong service offering.

Further, we advise executives in service companies with mediocre names to consider all possible options in improving the presented brand. A new name may not be the right medicine. The existing name, though flawed, may provide enough familiarity, comfort, and credibility for customers and other stakeholders that these qualities simply should not be sacrificed. For example, Delta Airlines would be foolish to change its name, although technically "Delta" is at best an average name for a transportation company. Delta Airlines would need a much better reason than a bland-sounding name to give away the goodwill and reputation it has developed over the years.

On the other hand, Allegheny Airlines' name change to USAir was a masterstroke of good marketing. One problem was the regional connotation of "Allegheny" for an airline that was expanding its route structure dramatically and positioning itself as a national carrier. Another problem was the unpleasant nickname, "Agony Airlines," that passengers disappointed with the service derived from the Allegheny name. (Some readers probably will have another unpleasant nickname for USAir, an airline struggling with earnings at this writing. However, we doubt that readers, were they executives of USAir, would be willing to revert to Allegheny.) The name change to USAir was good medicine for the company when it was implemented. Today, the company requires a different, and stronger remedy to shore up its brand meaning.

Aside from the potential sacrifice of brand name "equity," name changes are expensive and logistically complex. A new name means new signs, new stationery, new billing statements, and new advertising. A new name may mean legal fees, consulting and design fees, and fees for translators searching for unintended meanings in other languages.

The bottom line: a new name can be risky and expensive medicine; marketers need to be deliberate and strategic, and do their research before deciding on a name change. The existing name presented in an innovative way through more media may be a better remedy.

BUILD ON WHAT EXISTS

Conditions sometimes dictate a clean break with the company's past and an entirely new identity. The Allegheny Airlines example is a case in point. The existing identity was incompatible with the company's strategy, and it was the breeding ground for negative connotation as well. The existing brand meaning was a strategic straightjacket, and a totally fresh start in branding was indicated.

However, a clean break with the past is often a bad idea. Given the heavy investment required to build and sustain brand awareness in services marketing, it is better to build on what exists and improve it whenever possible. Linking the new to the old is usually better than discarding the old; continuously improving the branding effort in small ways is preferable to long periods of complacency and then sudden bursts of newness.

Branding continuity through melding the old and new smoothly and logically often gives marketers the best of two worlds: the equity of the past and the excitement of the future. Renaming the combined Southern Bell and South Central Bell as BellSouth illustrates the guideline of building on what exists. So do the ingenious linkages between company brand and product brands at McDonald's, e.g., Egg McMuffins, Chicken McNuggets. So does the mid-1970s name change of First National City Bank to Citibank. And so does the brand extension philosophy at Marriott Corporation as the company has developed new product lines, e.g., Courtyard by Marriott and Marriott Suites.

INTERNALIZE THE BRAND

Service company employees can be the most powerful medium for conveying the brand to customers. More than any other communications medium, employees can breathe life, vitality, and personality into the brand. With their on-the-job performances, employees can transform for customers a verbal-visual brand into a verbal-visual-action brand. With their on-the-job performances, employees can *reinforce* the presented brand.

Internalizing the brand involves explaining and selling the brand to employees. It involves sharing with employees the research and strategy behind the presented brand. It involves creative communication of the brand to employees. It involves training employees in brand-strengthening behaviors. It involves rewarding and celebrating employees whose actions support the brand. Most of all, internalizing the brand involves *involving* employees in the care and nurturing of the brand.

Employees will not feel part of nor act out the brand unless they understand it and believe in it. Marketers need to verbalize and visualize the brand for employees, so that employees will verbalize and visualize the brand for customers. Brand internalization must be an ongoing process, just as brand building is an ongoing process with customers.

Pier 1 imports, one of America's fastest-growing specialty retail chains, includes in its branding the theme line "a place to discover." And indeed it is with 40 percent of its imported product assortment new each year. Thus, it is both appropriate and important that Pier 1 emphasizes in its salesperson training the need to allow customers to browse. If the customer is to be creative in reshaping the look of her home with Pier 1 merchandise, she should feel comfortable taking her time in the store. She should be able to wander the store without a salesperson hovering nearby with that "when are you going to buy something" look. Excellent service at Pier 1 is defined as letting the customer browse freely, unencumbered by aggressive selling behavior.

As discussed in the previous chapter, the trust company of Bank One Texas has implemented an unconditional service guarantee to underscore its commitment to service quality. Management is internalizing this commitment through a variety of conventional methods in the training, reward and recognition, and quality-improvement team areas. It is also using a decidedly *unconventional* approach: managers and nonmanagerial employees refer to one another as "service animals." In many other companies this reference would be considered trite or even crass, but in this company it has become a bonding symbol, a proud battle cry, an internal signature. When employees refer to one another as service animals—and they do so frequently—they are reminded of what their company stands for and what the company brand is supposed to mean to clients.

SUMMARY AND ACTION CHECKLIST

An effective branding strategy is not a panacea for service companies. A strong presented brand will not rescue a weak service. What a strong presented brand will do is give a competitive service a marketing edge.

Brand meaning, the customers' snapshot impression and classification of the firm, is a function of brand presentation *and* service concept, quality, and value. The more customers are familiar with a firm's service offering, the more their perceptions of the service influence what the company brand means to them. The role of branding in service firms is to strongly communicate a strong service; the role is *not* to compensate for a weak service. As with other forms of evidence, the brand must bring energy and vitality to the marketing strategy.

The brand name tests discussed in this chapter—distinctiveness, relevance, memorability, and flexibility—also apply to the branding of goods. And the points we made about brand cohesiveness and consistency fit goods branding, too. The principal difference is that services marketers must brand the company, because in services it is the company that customers "buy." Services marketers also may attempt to brand individual service-products but these efforts will do little good unless the company brand is effective.

Services marketers must find a way to differentiate a company that markets more or less invisible products, to "package" through communications and other evidence that which cannot be packaged literally. Branding is a critical tool.

Here is an "action checklist" of branding questions that managers in a firm should ask:

1. *Are we proactive in presenting a strong company brand to our customers (and other stakeholders)?* Do we talk at the senior management level about branding? Do our managers view our company brand as a critical marketing asset? Do our nonmanagerial employees?

2. *How does our company name rate on the tests of distinctiveness, relevance, memorability, and flexibility?* On which of these criteria is our name weakest? Should we take action on this or any other weakness in our name?

3. *Do we use to full advantage branding elements other than the company name?* Are we asking too little from other branding elements, such as symbols and slogans?

4. *Is our presented brand cohesive?* Are we effectively integrating the verbal and visual elements? Do all elements of our brand work together?

5. *Do we apply our brand consistently across all media?* Do we have mechanisms in place to protect the fidelity with which our brand is presented?

6. *Do we use all possible media to present our brand?* Are we creative in identifying brand-presentation opportunities? Are we tapping every opportunity to "show and tell?"

7. *Do we recognize the influence of the service offering on brand meaning?* Do we as managers understand that strong branding techniques cannot rescue a weak service?

8. *Do we base our branding decisions on research?* Do we know how our brand compares to competitive brands? Do we know what our brand means to customers and others, and why?

9. *Are we respectful of what exists when we change our brand or add new brands?* Do we build on our branding goodwill, or are we quick to seek fresh beginnings?

10. *Do we internalize our branding?* Do we market our brand to our employees so they will market it to our customers? Do our employees understand and believe in our brand? Do they feel it is their brand?

8

◇◆◇

Marketing to Existing Customers

Service firms can increase market share three ways: attract more new customers, do more business with existing customers, and reduce customer attrition. Companies that direct marketing resources at existing customers address two of the three possibilities: they increase the opportunity to expand customer relationships and decrease the chances that customers will stray to competitors.

Marketing to attract new customers is merely an intermediate step in the marketing process; for most service firms the more significant marketing opportunity occurs *after* prospects become customers. The prospect-turned-customer has made a commitment to the company by selecting it—by deciding for some reason that the company's service represents the best available alternative. Further, the one-time prospect has invested money and time to become a customer (just as the company has invested resources to create this transformation).

What the company does to nurture the relationship with the customer, to build it, to strengthen it, is crucial to the company's marketing effectiveness and efficiency. To work hard to attract new customers and then to be complacent in strengthening the relationship makes little sense. Yet companies commonly make this mistake. The marketing director of a major bank told us: "Nearly 80 percent of our monthly sales are to existing customers, yet we suffer from attrition which often equals our new account activity." Unfortunately, this bank's dilemma is not unique.

The failure is in what Michael O'Connor calls the "second act." The firm focuses on attracting customers into the fold (the first act) but pays little or no attention to what should be done to keep customers coming back (the second act).[1] In his article, O'Connor introduces his former teacher, Daniel Carmichael, who taught students the "Leaky Barrel Theory of Marketing." O'Connor recounts:

> Carmichael began his lecture by drawing a picture of a barrel on the blackboard. He then drew a number of holes in the barrel and gave them titles: rudeness, out of stock, poor service, untrained employees, poor quality, poor selection, poor value, etc. He drew streams of water gushing from each hole, and likened them to customers. The good professor pointed out to his students that in order to maintain a business such as this one, the company must constantly "pour" new customers into the top of the barrel—an expensive and never-ending process. He added that the successful company plugged the holes in its barrel and lost far fewer customers.[2]

O'Connor's "second act" analogy and his teacher's "leaky barrel" theory are consistent with the distinction we made in the previous chapter between the presented brand and brand meaning. The presented brand attracts new customers, but it is brand meaning, based on the customer's overall experiences with the firm, that strengthens or weakens the initial company-customer bond. A company brand that doesn't mean the right things to customers is Professor Carmichael's leaky barrel.

CREATING TRUE CUSTOMERS

For most services, existing customers represent by far the best opportunities for profit growth. If customers have an ongoing or periodic desire for a service and can obtain the service from more than one source, then no marketing concept will be more important in the firm than relationship marketing. *Relationship marketing concerns attracting, developing, and retaining customer relationships*. Its central tenet is the creation of "true customers"—customers who are glad they selected a firm, who perceive they are receiving value and feel valued, who are likely to buy additional services from the firm, and who are unlikely to defect to a competitor.

True customers are the most profitable of all customers. They spend more money with the firm on a per-year basis and they stay with the firm for more years. They spread favorable word-of-mouth information about the firm, and they may even be willing to pay a premium price for the benefits the service offers.[3]

Moreover, companies with many true customers typically have lower marketing costs than companies with significant customer churn. This churn results in costs for (1) persuading prospects unfamiliar with a company's services and their benefits to become customers; and (2) providing start-up services to new customers such as new account paperwork. In addition, true customers' word-of-mouth advertising bolsters the impact of paid advertising, effectively lowering the cost of advertising.

Reichheld and Sasser conclude from their research that, depending upon the industry, companies can improve profits from 25 percent to 85 percent by reducing customer defections just 5 percent.[4] Consultant Laura Liswood urges managers who question the value of relationship marketing to calculate the lifetime value of their customers. She estimates, for example, that the lifetime value of a supermarket customer averages $250,000.[5]

CUSTOMERS BENEFIT TOO

The benefits of relationship marketing are not one-sided. Many service customers would like to oblige firms that covet true customers. As Czepiel and Gilmore point out, because of their intangibility, heterogeneity, and interaction intensity, services have an inherently greater capacity than goods to create customer loyalty.[6] The invisible, variable nature of services gives auto repair, hair styling, real estate, health care, accounting, marketing research and many other types of service firms a decided competitive advantage with existing customers if they perform the service well and earn the customers' confidence. The interaction intensity of many services offers customers the opportunity to observe the provider's behavior and solidify their perceptions.[7]

In customer focus group research that we conducted with our colleague, Valarie Zeithaml, it was clear that many service customers want to be "relationship customers" of the firms serving them. They want ongoing, personalized relationships with the same representatives. They want these representatives to contact them, rather than always having to initiate the contact themselves. They want a "partner"—someone who knows them and who cares about them.

Customers' desires for closer, more personalized relationships with service providers were evident not only in the interviews for such services as insurance and truck leasing, which are ongoing by nature, but also for hotel and repair services, which are provided intermittently. The following comments illustrate the pervasiveness of customers' expectations for service relationships:

BUSINESS INSURANCE CUSTOMER: They should be a partner and more actively give me advice on what my calculated risks are. When they are a partner, our money is their money too.

TRUCK LEASING CUSTOMER: I would like them to be a distant extension of my company. They should take care of the details.

BUSINESS EQUIPMENT REPAIR CUSTOMER: You need to know the service tech. I should be able to call him directly. I want to know the tech on a one-to-one basis.

AUTO INSURANCE CUSTOMER: Agents should come back to you and ask you if you need more coverage as your assets increase.

HOTEL CUSTOMER: When employees remember and recognize you as a regular customer, you feel really good.

Unfortunately, relationship-seeking customers are frequently disappointed. Despite the favorable profit impact of relationship marketing, the preponderance of evidence from our research indicates *unrealized* customer relationships. An auto repair customer complained: "They don't keep the service writers long enough for customers to develop a relationship with them. Every time you come in there is a whole new crew." A business insurance customer stated: "We lose contact with the company as soon as we sign off on the policy." An auto insurance customer said: "I've never had an agent contact me. All I see is a bill."[8]

FROM CUSTOMERS TO CLIENTS

If relationship marketing is so beneficial to company and customer alike, why are so few American service companies practicing excellent relationship marketing as we write this book? Marketing effectively to existing customers clearly pays and yet our research indicates considerable room for improvement.

One factor contributing to the mediocrity of current relationship marketing efforts is the common assumption that adding new customers is the quickest route to improved profitability. This assumption, coupled with the short-term profit emphasis characteristic of

American business, is why the goal of attracting more new customers usually holds sway over the goal of doing a better job serving and selling existing customers. That existing customers typically offer richer profits more quickly than do new customers is hidden by accounting practices that do not fully reflect the costs of acquiring and serving new customers. Nor do most executives appreciate the stream of value that *true* customers generate. As Reichheld and Sasser write: "Today's accounting systems do not capture the value of a loyal customer."[9]

New customers generate cash flow if not profits and managers are expected to generate higher sales every quarter. It seems right to focus the most attention and resources on other companies' customers rather than on one's own customers. The problem is that relationship marketing is done with customers, not prospects, and is incompatible with a quick-fix mentality in its highest and most profitable forms. The principal reason for attracting new customers is to proceed with the slow, plodding work of building trust and demonstrating competence—the cornerstones of relationship building. Relationship marketing is about fundamentals, not flash, substance, not style.

THREE LEVELS OF RELATIONSHIP MARKETING

Relationship marketing can be practiced on one of three levels, depending on the type and number of bonds that a company uses to foster customer loyalty. The higher the level at which relationship marketing is practiced, the higher the potential payoff. Exhibit 8–1 summarizes the three levels.

Level One Relationship Marketing. Level one relationship marketing is often referred to as either "frequency" or "retention" marketing. At level one, marketers primarily use pricing incentives to encourage customers to bring the firm more of their business. Banks may offer higher interest rates for larger or longer-duration account balances; hotel chains may offer free or discounted travel services to frequent guests; supermarkets may give cash rebates, electronic green stamps, or extra coupons to regular customers. As we write this book, level one relationship marketing programs are growing rapidly. For example, of 9,800 food retailers surveyed in 1989, 1,372 offered some form of frequent-buyer program, an increase of about 24 percent compared to 1988.[10]

Unfortunately, many level one marketers will be disappointed with

Exhibit 8–1 The Three Levels of Relationship Marketing

Level	Type of Bond(s)	Marketing Orientation	Degree of Service Customization	Primary Marketing Mix Element	Potential for Sustained Competitive Differentiation
One	Financial	Customer	Low	Price	Low
Two	Financial and Social	Client	Medium	Personal Communications	Medium
Three	Financial, Social, and Structural	Client	Medium to High	Service Delivery	High

the long-term if not the short-term results from their programs. Price is the most easily imitated element of the marketing mix and in and of itself does not offer a sustainable competitive advantage. Airline frequent flyer programs offer a good example.

In 1983 American Airlines introduced its AAdvantage program, enabling frequent travelers to accumulate mileage redeemable for free or upgraded travel. The AAdvantage program was targeted to about 3 percent of all air travelers. What American's management did not anticipate was (1) the broad appeal of free travel to the public (American had 11 million AAdvantage members by 1990);[11] (2) competitors' perceived need to respond in kind (24 of 27 major airline carriers had frequent flier programs by 1986);[12] and (3) the virtual impossibility of stopping such a program once underway.

Airlines are supposed to sell tickets, not give them away. Frequent flyer programs, designed to encourage brand loyalty among business travelers, have had the unwanted effects of reducing demand for paid tickets and limiting available seats for fare-paying passengers, especially to popular vacation spots like Hawaii.[13] Frequent flyer programs clearly have encouraged some brand loyalty and offered additional benefits (for example, mailing lists of prime customers for promotional and research purposes). What they have not done is *differentiate* the sponsoring airlines for frequent travelers to the degree that justifies the costs and drawbacks. The frequent flyer concept, essentially pricing benefits for better customers, is simply too easily imitated.

Marketers seeking to build the strongest possible customer relationships need to establish bonds that are important to customers but difficult for competitors to imitate. Free travel awards pass the importance test but flunk the differentiation test. And because many of the frequency marketing programs in other industries are structured like the airline frequent flyer programs, we are not optimistic about their long-term prospects.

Level Two Relationship Marketing. Level two marketers go beyond pricing incentives in building relationships. They do not ignore the importance of price competition but seek to build social bonds on top of any financial bonds that may exist. Level two marketing emphasizes personalized service delivery and the transformation of customers into clients. Donnelly, Berry, and Thompson, in their book *Marketing Financial Services,* describe the differences between customers and clients:

> Customers may be nameless to the institution; clients cannot be nameless. Customers are served as part of the mass or as part of larger segments; clients are served on an individual basis. Customers are statistics; their needs are reflected on computer printout summaries. Clients are entities in and of themselves; specifics about them—background data, services used, special requirements—are captured in a data base. Customers are served by anyone who happens to be available; clients are served—at least for nonroutine needs—by the professional . . . assigned to them.[14]

Level two marketers stress staying in touch with clients, learning about their wants and needs, customizing the relationships based on what is learned, and continually reselling the benefits of the relationship. Level two marketing is as much a product of soul as science; it couples person-to-person marketing with company-to-person marketing.

Social bonding usually will not overcome significant price or service weaknesses. It can, however, encourage clients to remain in a relationship in the absence of strong reasons to shift; it can give a company opportunity for responding to service snafus or competitor entreaties before a customer defects.[15]

In a study of the quality of salesperson-client relationships in the life insurance industry, Crosby, Evans, and Cowles found a significant effect of relational selling behaviors on relationship quality—

defined as client trust in, and satisfaction with, the salesperson. Relationship quality, in turn, had a significant positive influence on clients' anticipation of future interactions with the salesperson. Relationship selling behaviors include seeking out clients to stay in touch and reassess their needs; providing personal touches like cards and gifts; confiding in clients and getting them to confide back; and demonstrating a cooperative, responsive service attitude.[16]

One service company that demonstrates relational selling behaviors is the University National Bank & Trust Company in Palo Alto, California. Starting business in 1980, UNB&T had grown to more than $200 million in deposits ten years later with annual earnings consistently greater than peer banks. From the start, the bank sought clients rather than customers, insisting that all clients have a checking account as the basis for building relationships. Relationships are built on the foundation of mutual commitment and UNB&T's policy of requiring a checking account reflects its philosophy of making such a commitment to each client and expecting one in return. Founder, chairman, and CEO Carl Schmitt states:

> We are solitary in not offering products, but in focusing on relationships. I don't know of any bank that would turn down someone with a million dollar deposit because he didn't have a checking account at the bank, but we would. All our deposits are core deposits and we have never violated that rule. It's very key to our culture.[17]

Personalized service is paramount at UNB&T. At each of its two offices, banking teams of lending and deposit officers are assigned to commercial and trust clients. All contact employees, including tellers, refer to clients by name when serving them. When visiting the bank, clients receive free shoe shines, buy postage stamps at cost, and use adding machines and pens that are *not* chained to the desk. Each June the bank invites its clients to place an order for free Walla Walla sweet onions. In 1989, it gave away 17,400 pounds of the onions to its clients. Also, each year clients receive a handsome pictorial book in appreciation for the past year's patronage. This note accompanied the seventh book:

> *Happy Anniversary!*
> *We have greatly appreciated your business over the past year.*
> *Our goal is to provide "a Different Experience in Banking." I*

hope that we have done this for you and that we may be favored with your business for many years to come.
Best wishes,
Carl J. Schmitt
Chairman
Herbert C. Foster
President

The University National Bank and Trust Company uses social bonding to build durable relationships. It uses giveaways like the onions in a social context to express friendship and gratitude for the relationship. As part of a much broader fabric of client experiences with the bank, the giveaways have social meaning rather than financial meaning and thus are far more difficult for competitors to imitate.

Level Three Relationship Marketing. Level three marketers solidify relationships with structural bonds in addition to social and financial bonds. Structural bonds are created by providing services that are valuable to clients and not readily available from other sources; these services are often technology-based and intended to help clients be more efficient or productive. The services are designed into the delivery system rather than being dependent upon the relation-building behaviors of individual personnel—hence, the use of the term "structural."

When well-executed, structural bonds raise the clients' costs for switching to competitors (because they give up more). Structural solutions increase the benefits of switching for competitors' customers (because they gain more elsewhere). In particular, structural bonds add a nonpricing dynamic to augment any existing social bonding in the face of difficult price competition. Turnbull and Wilson make this point well:

> Social bonding between all of the buyers and sales people may be high, but social bonding will not maintain the sales relationships in the face of large price differences. Professional buyers must justify price premiums, and good personal relationships may only justify a small premium. It is easier for buyers to resist a lower price from a competitor who does not offer the technical service that the buyer requires. The structural bond that is created by the seller investing in technical support binds the medium sized customer to the seller.[18]

McKesson Corporation, a pharmaceutical distribution company, offers a good example of level three relationship marketing. Investing millions of dollars to develop an electronic data interchange capability with independent pharmacists, McKesson's business grew from $1 billion to $6 billion in the 1980s. McKesson developed computerized services to help smaller retailers compete with drug chains in inventory management, pricing, credit, and other tasks. These services include *Economost* and *Econoscan,* processes enabling retailers to use a hand-held computer and optical character scanner for electronic order entry, inventory control, and shelf management; *Econocharge,* a store credit-card system; *Econoclaim,* a system for processing prescription information and insurance claims; and *Pharmaserve,* an in-store computer system.[19]

McKesson's strategy illustrates the bonding power of structural solutions to clients' keenly felt needs. Focusing resources on helping its target market of smaller drugstore retailers compete with major drugstore chains, McKesson created formal linkages with clients that made switching to other suppliers far more difficult.

On the surface, structural bonding seems less applicable to consumer services marketing than to industrial services marketing. In fact this is not the case. The key to level three marketing is to provide *value-adding* services that are difficult or expensive for clients to provide for themselves and that are not readily available elsewhere. Because industrial services often are technically complex and require substantial investments to obtain and use (such as computer or telephone system installation), they lend themselves to the type of structural partnering evident in the McKesson example.

Nonetheless, structural bonds can be created in consumer services marketing. It is a question of cleverness, creativity, and commitment to the philosophy of relationship marketing. What McKesson has done in a broad sense is to create systems that help clients be more successful. Consumer marketers can do this too.

In 1977, Merrill-Lynch launched its Cash Management Account and created one of the biggest success stories ever in financial services marketing. What the CMA offered consumers was an automatic sweep of the proceeds from stock or bond sales into a money-market fund so that consumers' funds were continually earning interest. Consumers could then access these funds by writing a check or using a debit card. If the account balances were insufficient to cover such transactions, credit collateralized by securities was automatically extended.

Upscale consumer-investors liked the convenience, simplicity, and flexibility of this all-in-one account summarized each month on an integrated statement. They also liked the earning power of an account in which funds were never idle. Yet it took several years before competitors could develop the technology to offer similar services. By the fall of 1982, Merrill-Lynch had more than 750,000 CMA clients with an average account balance of $67,000.[20] By the fall of 1990 these numbers had more than doubled to 1,600,000 CMA clients with an average account balance of $155,000.

Another consumer services illustration of structural bonding is American Airlines' AAdvantage Gold program targeted to the top 2 to 3 percent of all AAdvantage members based on accrued mileage. Capitalizing on its highly sophisticated SABRE information system, American offers its best clients service extras that many competitors are unable or unwilling to duplicate at this time. These extras include the Gold Hot Line, an exclusive toll-free reservation/information telephone line; blocking the most desirable coach seats for AAdvantage Gold members until two days prior to departure; keeping the middle seat next to a Gold member unoccupied whenever possible; pre-boarding with first-class passengers; upgrades to the first-class cabin; and a personal travel profile maintained in the SABRE system. With AAdvantage Gold, American Airlines has created a package of small benefits that (1) are more likely to be noticed, used, and valued by frequent business travelers; (2) offer prestige and exclusivity that basic frequent flier programs no longer offer; and (3) are available only with continued, heavy patronage. With AAdvantage Gold, American has created a structural response to the stress-filled reality of frequent airline travel and to the ego needs of full-fare executives traveling on the same airplane with high school students on a field trip.

THE ART OF RELATIONSHIP MARKETING

The challenge facing relationship marketers is to create true customers* who perceive that they have a relationship with the firm and who value the relationship. This requires benefits that are important to customers and difficult for competitors to duplicate. Level two

---

*Having made the distinction between customers and clients in the last section, we will use the generic term "customer" as a writing convenience except when specifically addressing the customer-client distinction.

relationship marketing provides a greater opportunity to deliver these benefits than level one and level three a greater opportunity than level two.

The art of relationship marketing revolves around the delivery of value to customers. Value is the glue that binds company and customer together. Value reflects the total benefit customers receive for the total "cost" they incur.[21] To illustrate, the basic service of a haircut is only one component of benefit. The decor and comfort of the shop, the personableness of the hair stylist, the grooming tips the hair stylist might suggest—these also help define the benefit side of the value equation.

Similarly, price is only one component of total cost. Total cost represents the full burden customers must bear to obtain the service—for example, the inconvenience of a distant shop location, or the unpleasant atmosphere in a small waiting room where the receptionist chain smokes.

One of the most important lessons for services marketers to remember is that low price and high value are not synonymous. Low price may be a part of a strong value offer but not necessarily. Dr. Laura Popper, the Manhattan pediatrician we quoted in Chapter 6, told us:

> I have a one-person practice; it is very personal. I know the families of my patients and what's going on with them. My patients range in age from birth to 27 years, as some don't want to leave even as they get older. You are a better doctor if you treat more than just symptoms and diseases. People need to be seen as a whole, not as individual pieces of a puzzle. If you don't understand who you serve, you don't serve them.

In our interview with Dr. Popper we never asked her about the fees she charges, or how they compare with the fees of other nearby pediatricians. It seemed to us tangential to what she had to teach us about services marketing. Dr. Popper is a strong relationship marketer precisely because she offers more than price.

It is because the perception of value drives relationships that quality service is so important. Central to the service benefits and costs that customers perceive is the reliability, tangibles, responsiveness, assurance, and empathy of the service. From discount stores to banking institutions, from telephone companies to accounting firms, from computer software establishments to beauty salons, delivering value to customers defines the potential for relationship marketing, and delivering high quality service directly influences the potential for value.

Three manifestations of quality service that are particularly relevant to relationship building are:

- Fair play
- One-on-one marketing
- Service augmentation

FAIR PLAY

Customer-company relationships require trust, not unlike other types of relationships. And trust requires fair play. Few customers wish to build or continue a relationship with a firm they perceive to be unfair.

Fairness involves creating a level playing field on which both seller and buyer can realize their objectives, listening to customers and being sensitive to their concerns, disclosing accurate information relevant to any transaction, and keeping promises—seller to buyer and buyer to seller.

In our ongoing service quality research program, we have seen much evidence of the resentment and mistrust that occurs when customers perceive unfair practices. A hotel customer complained: "You get charged when you don't show up but there is no reverse penalty when they don't have your guaranteed room." A car repair customer stated: "The dealer will do as little as possible." A business insurance customer said: "The purpose of insurance companies is to insure, but they have so many exclusions from A to Z that you don't know what the hell is covered."[22]

These comments are typical of many others we have heard in the course of our studies; they point to missed opportunity to build true customer relationships through mutual trust. Instead of trying to protect the company from unfair customers (for example, heavy overbooking to cancel out the effects of no-shows) service companies should cater to those customers who are fair (the vast majority) and deal stringently with those who are not. Instead of doing as little as possible for customers to cut costs, firms should focus on what is most valuable to customers and do as much as possible for them. Instead of trying to keep customers from learning about a service's comparative disadvantages, the firm should correct the weaknesses and enlighten customers.

Marketers who want to practice relationship marketing must be prepared to subject every policy and every strategy to a fairness test. They must be prepared to level the playing field. They must be prepared to ask not only: "Is it legal?" but also "Is it right?"

ONE-ON-ONE MARKETING

Smart services marketers effectively resist the temptation of taking existing customers for granted. Instead, they strive to create a marketing culture in which existing customers are treated as though they were new prospects. Smart services marketers woo existing customers by staying in touch with them and by personalizing the service. They treat the customer as a market segment of one.

One-on-one marketing has several requisites. First, customers must have access to service. If they are to have a relationship with a firm, they need to be able to initiate contact and receive service as their need arises. Access is fundamental to relationship building. General Electric spends $10 million per year to keep the GE Answer Center running 24 hours a day, 365 days a year. The computerized information system supporting the Center's service representatives contains answers to 750,000 questions that customers might ask. Service representatives receive 100 hours of update and refresher training each year.[23] N. Powell Taylor, manager of the Center, states: "We're trying to build a bond with the customer—a bond that'll last many years and give us a real competitive advantage."[24]

A second requisite of one-on-one marketing is that communications should be two-way—company-initiated as well as customer-initiated. Customers are less likely to perceive that they have a relationship with a particular company if they always have to initiate the contact.[25] Regular company-initiated contacts with customers are important to assess their perceptions of the service, identify new or changing requirements, resell the benefits of the relationship, and say thank you. PHH Corporation requires that its account managers hold annual reviews with each account. The appropriate PHH vice president also attends these reviews. The meeting is used to discuss the services provided the client during the past year, reinforce the value added that has been delivered, establish what the client would like to accomplish during the coming year, agree on how the client will judge PHH's performance in the areas noted, and agree on the issues to be discussed at the next meeting. In addition to these annual account review meetings, PHH also assigns a member of senior management (including the company chairman) to call on existing customers several times a year and to prepare reports based on these visits for the president of the appropriate operating unit and the account representative.

A third requisite is the organizational and informational means to efficiently tailor service to customers' specific requirements. The key word is "efficiently." Cost-effective customization depends on the right organizational structure and technology. Over the past 15 years an increasing number of banks have reorganized the retail side of the bank to assign "personal bankers" to some or all customers. Personal bankers typically administer the relationship for assigned customers, provide advice, solve problems, keep customers informed, and sell additional services.[26] When personal banking is executed well, customers have a banker as well as a bank and they become clients.

With personal banking and other forms of one-on-one marketing, precise, relevant customer information is essential. For example, a hotel could build an information system that captures guest preferences based on data from a guest questionnaire. Using this information, the hotel could efficiently personalize and enhance service in various ways, from automatic check-in when guests arrive at the property to pre-stocking the rooms with their preferred whiskey.

Staples, the Boston-based office products retailer, offers its customers membership cards to use when they pay for their purchases. To obtain the card, customers must provide background information, including mailing address, on an application. While the membership card gives customers access to discounts and special promotions, it allows Staples to track an individual customer's frequency of visits, plus the size and type of purchases made.[27] This system also gives Staples a way to customize the relationship through direct mail promotions of merchandise to customers who have purchased in that category and invitations to special seminars or product demonstrations.

A fourth requisite for one-on-one marketing is a management system in which service providers find it worthwhile to cater to existing customers. Service providers must be *willing* to deliver one-on-one marketing in addition to being *able* to. New ideas for measuring and rewarding employees' performance may be necessary. For example, many insurance companies reward their agents handsomely for selling new policies but meagerly or not at all for serving existing customers; this effectively discourages agents from being attentive to current policyholders. In these companies, managers have engineered conflict between selling and serving, diminishing the opportunity for relationship-based service.[28]

MBNA America, a large bank credit card operation, annually retains 95 percent of its customers compared to an 88 percent rate for its competitors. One reason for MBNA's success is its management system of measuring the factors that most affect customer satisfaction (response time to written or telephone inquiries and error-free statements), and distributing bonuses that can amount to 20 percent of total compensation when employee groups achieve performance standards in these areas.[29]

SERVICE AUGMENTATION

Another contributor to relationship building is service augmentation—a topic we have referred to indirectly throughout the chapter. Service augmentation involves incorporating "extras" into the service offer to differentiate it from competitive offerings.[30] In effect, marketers augment the primary service with additional services to make the total offer more appealing. The trick is to identify extras that are valued by customers, not easily copied by competitors, and financially and operationally feasible.

The potential benefits of service augmentation strategies are often blunted because they are so easily copied by competitors. Our earlier discussion of the airline frequent flyer programs illustrates this point. American Airlines' AAdvantage program would have been a great idea if only the other airlines had stayed away from similar programs. But of course this was not to be. American Airlines was too big and powerful a carrier for competitors to ignore its efforts to build loyalty among frequent-traveler executives—the most profitable of all travel segments.

We see the same pattern of imitative augmentation in upscale hotel chains. What started out as mints on the pillow has led to a blizzard of toiletries in the bathroom, a newspaper in the morning, and even a terry-cloth robe hanging in the closet (with the obligatory printed card discouraging guests from taking it home). These are nice amenities but their value in differentiating one hotel from another is doubtful. These amenities are now so widely available that they have become "standard." Guests expect the hotels to offer them and thus there is no surprise when they do. And no loyalty because they do.

So what is the answer? What can marketers do to achieve genuine differentiation through service augmentation? The answer is to move beyond level one marketing, building social and, if possible, structural extras on top of any financial or "free" extras. This is the magic of companies like Stew Leonard's or University National Bank and Trust. The *whole* company is different from competitors—the ambience, the attitude, and the culture—and efforts at augmentation (from Stew Leonard's animal farm in front of the store to UNB&T's Walla Walla onions) reinforce an overall pattern that creates uniqueness. Service augmentation efforts that fit a company's culture and reflect social and structural bonding, not just financial bonding, hold the greatest potential for relationship marketing. Such efforts are most likely to be valued by customers and least likely to be copied effectively by competitors.

Exhibit 8–2 summarizes the key building blocks of relationship marketing and the linkages between them. Perceived service quality and the types of bonds a company offers its customers are key drivers of perceived value—the benefits versus costs comparisons that customers make. Perceived value, in turn, determines the level, and strength, of company-customer relationships. The broken-line arrows in the exhibit signify secondary interconnections between the corresponding constructs.

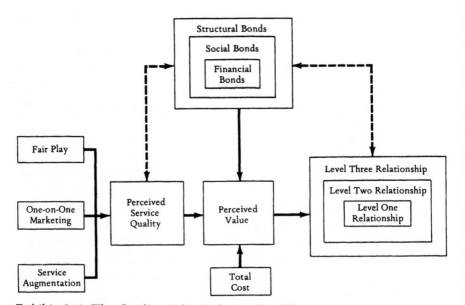

Exhibit 8–2 The Quality-Value-Relationship Chain

SUMMARY AND ACTION CHECKLIST

Service businesses can increase market share by attracting more new customers, doing more business with existing customers, and reducing the loss of customers. Formally marketing to existing customers addresses two of the three possibilities. New customer marketing is an intermediate step in the marketing process; what a firm does after it converts a prospect to a customer will go a long way toward determining that customer's ultimate profitability.

In this chapter, we argue the merits of relationship marketing which can be practiced on one of three levels. The higher the level at which relationship marketing is practiced, the greater the opportunity to create "true" customers, the most profitable of all customers. Level one relationship marketing emphasizes financial incentives, and it is the most easily imitated by competitors. Level two adds the dimension of social bonding through the personalization of the relationship and is less easily duplicated by competitors. Level three adds structural solutions to customer problems and holds the most potential for competitive differentiation. Marketers that provide all three types of bonds—financial, social, and structural—and generally deliver a high quality of service are most likely to deliver the level of value that creates true customers. Three manifestations of high quality service that contribute directly to relationship building are fair play, one-on-one marketing and service augmentation.

Here is an action checklist of questions that managers should ask concerning the effectiveness of the firm's existing customer marketing:

1. *Have we calculated the lifetime value of a customer?* Do we know the profit impact of reducing our customer defection rate by just 5 percent? Have we communicated this information to our people? Do they know the value of existing customers to the firm and to themselves?

2. *Do we plan our existing customer marketing as carefully as we plan our new customer marketing?* Do we think in terms of creating *true customers* or just customers? Do we think in terms of *relationship marketing* or just marketing?

3. *Do we stress value over price in our marketing?* Do we over-rely on pricing incentives and then wonder why we have so little customer loyalty? Do we feel that we have to buy customer loyalty?

4. *Do we work hard to establish social bonds with our customers?* Do we do all that we can do to stay in touch with customers, resell the relationship, and say "thank you"? Do we encourage relational selling behaviors by how we recruit, train, measure, and compensate customer-contact personnel? Do we focus enough energy on the "two C's" of services marketing—communication and customization?

5. *Do we seek structural solutions to customer problems?* Do we actively seek to raise the switching costs to our customers and the switching benefits to our competitors' customers?

6. *Do we prize fairness in our company?* Is fairness at the core of our company culture? When we make decisions that affect customers do we make sure these decisions pass the fairness test?

7. *Do we focus enough on competitive differentiation?* Do we try to differentiate our *whole* company or do we rely mostly on one or two elements of the marketing mix to be distinctive?

9

◇◇◇

Marketing to Employees

For most services, the server cannot be separated from the service. The accountant is a significant part of the accounting service, the physician a significant part of the medical service. In reality, customers "buy" the people when they buy a service. Service, after all, is a performance and the performance is often labor-intensive.

Thus, for labor-intensive service firms especially, the quality of employees influences the quality of service which, in turn, influences the effectiveness of services marketing. To practice services marketing successfully, firms must practice *internal marketing* successfully. They must market to their own employees and to employee prospects, competing as imaginatively and aggressively for internal customers as for external customers.

Internal marketing is attracting, developing, motivating, and retaining qualified employees through job-products that satisfy their needs. Internal marketing is the *philosophy* of treating employees as customers—indeed, "wooing" employees as First Chicago's Linda Cooper puts it—and it is the *strategy* of shaping job-products to fit human needs.

The ultimate goal of internal marketing is to encourage effective marketing behavior; the ultimate goal is to build an organization of marketers willing and able to create true customers for the firm. The ultimate strategy of internal marketing is to create true customers of employees. As Hyatt Hotels' Susan Wall puts it: "A knowledgeable, satisfied employee is our best marketing agent. . . . We treat our employees the way we want them to treat our guests."[1]

PRACTICING INTERNAL MARKETING

Thinking like a marketer cannot be restricted to external marketing. By satisfying the needs of its internal customers, a firm enhances its ability to satisfy the needs of its external customers. In this chapter, we present seven essentials in the practice of internal marketing (Exhibit 9–1).

COMPETE FOR TALENT

Hiring the best possible people to perform the service is a key factor in services marketing. Yet many service companies act as though this were not the case. Many companies have ill-defined or woefully low standards for the personnel they hire. They involve few employees in the recruiting, interviewing, and selection process, sometimes

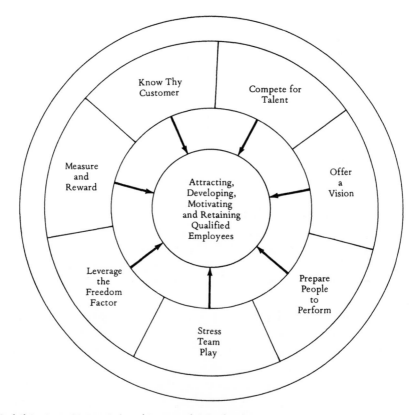

Exhibit 9–1 Essentials of Internal Marketing

delegating these tasks entirely to the personnel department. They tolerate incredibly high employee turnover rates, assuming this is a fact of life they cannot change.

One of the principal causes of poor service quality is hiring the wrong people to perform the service. In a large, empirical study we conducted with customer-contact employees from five major service firms, we found that employees who felt their units were not meeting service standards also felt their company was not hiring people qualified to do their jobs.[2]

Why do so many executives permit the wrong people to carry the company flag in front of customers? Part of the answer is the failure to think and act like a marketer when it comes to human resource issues. Marketing is used by most firms to compete for *sales* market share but not *talent* market share. Read the look-alike employment ads in the fine print in a local newspaper. Is this an effective way to compete for talent? The same firms that compete intensely and imaginatively for customers compete meekly and mundanely for employees.[3]

A Challenging Market. If ever there was a time for service firms to compete more effectively for talent, that time is now. The service sector is experiencing a labor-force shortfall that will intensify in the years immediately ahead. An expansion of service-sector jobs and an elevation of the skills required for these jobs are occurring just as the labor pool of young adults to assume these positions is shrinking. Moreover, many of the young adults who are available do not possess the required educational background and skills.[4]

The fastest growing job categories projected for the 1990s are in the service sector as shown in Exhibit 9–2. Virtually all of these high-growth job categories require independent thinking ability and many require technical skills training. With the baby boomers (people born between 1946 and 1964) having only about half as many children as their parents did,[5] with one million American youth dropping out of school each year,[6] and with only one-fourth of a group of 21- to 24-year-old whites able to decipher a bus schedule in a Department of Education study (the ratio was even worse for Hispanics and blacks),[7] there are simply not enough qualified employment candidates to satisfy the service sector's appetite in the next 10 years and beyond. The service firms that turn their marketing prowess to the labor market will fare best in the talent wars that lie ahead.

Thinking Like a Marketer. Here is what we recommend: Aim high, use multiple methods, cast a wide net, and segment the market. It is

Exhibit 9–2 Fastest Growing Job Categories for the 1990s

Biggest Percentage Growth

	Number of Workers (in thousands)		Percentage Change
	1988	2000	1988-2000
Paralegals	83	145	75.3%
Medical assistants	149	253	70.0
Home health aides	236	397	67.9
Radiologic technologists and technicians	132	218	66.0
Data processing equipment repairers	71	115	61.2
Medical records technicians	47	75	59.9
Medical secretaries	207	327	58.0
Physical therapists	68	107	57.0
Surgical technologists	35	55	56.4
Operations research analysts	55	85	55.4
Securities and financial services sales workers	200	309	54.8
Travel agents	142	219	54.1
Computer systems analysts	403	617	53.3
Physical and corrective therapy assistants	39	60	52.5
Social welfare service aides	91	138	51.5

Biggest Numerical Growth

	Number of Workers (in thousands)		Change in Number (in thousands)
	1988	2000	1988-2000
Salespersons, retail	3,834	4,564	730
Registered nurses	1,577	2,190	613
Janitors and cleaners, including maids	2,895	3,450	556
Waiters and waitresses	1,786	2,337	551
General managers and top executives	3,030	3,509	479
General office clerks	2,519	2,974	455
Secretaries, except legal and medical	2,903	3,288	385
Nursing aides, orderlies, and attendants	1,184	1,562	378
Truck drivers, light and heavy	2,399	2,768	369
Receptionists and information clerks	833	1,164	331
Cashiers	2,310	2,614	304
Guards	795	1,050	256
Computer programmers	519	769	250
Food counter, fountain and related	1,626	1,866	240
Food preparation workers	1,027	1,260	234

SOURCE: Adapted from Diane Crispell, "Workers in 2000," *American Demographics,* March 1990, p. 40. Based on Bureau of Labor Statistics projections.

tempting, given the intense competition for capable employees, to lower hiring standards. Smart internal marketers ignore this temptation and instead work harder than competitors to find the right people. Smart internal marketers aim high. They develop ideal candidate profiles for each type of position based on customer service expectations, and they use these profiles in recruiting candidates. They interview multiple candidates for one position, involve multiple employees in the interviewing process, and interview the more promising candidates on multiple occasions. They are tenacious in their pursuit of talent. Cadillac dealer Carl Sewell writes in his book, *Customers for Life:* "If you haven't talked to twenty-five people, you haven't looked hard enough."[8] Jim Daniel, president of the high-performing Friendly Bank in Oklahoma City, sounds the same theme:

> A continual challenge is finding people . . . who have the qualities necessary to provide the top-notch customer service that we require. Creative interviewing techniques must be utilized to obtain a clear picture of how the applicant truly feels about the public. Most applicants have had some degree of customer contact in previous employment. However, very few really *thrive* on customer contact. We look until we find that person.[9]

Using a variety of methods to reach prospective employees is also important. Firms seeking new employees need not use only classified advertising in newspapers, need not use only newspapers when advertising, and need not use only advertising when recruiting. Company-sponsored career fairs, tuition assistance for students who work while attending college, and employee-recruit-an-employee programs with finder fees or other incentives are just a few of the possibilities. In 1990 JCPenney employed more than 900 college students as summer interns with the objective of attracting at least 30 percent of them into full-time employment upon graduation.

Creative internal marketers also capitalize on the opportunities that demographic diversity brings, recruiting more women, minorities, seniors, disabled people, and immigrants. Pizza Hut is hiring approximately 1,500 disabled people each year, tapping into a pool of millions of disabled Americans who indicate in surveys that they wish to join the labor force.[10] Wal-Mart employs more than 10,000 people aged 65 or older as this book goes to press. Von Johnston, Director of Wal-Mart's People Division, states: "If you are not including the senior citizen in your human resources planning, you are missing the boat."[11]

Casting a wide net for new employees demands increased attention to internal market segmentation. The greater the heterogeneity of the labor pool, the greater the need to accommodate it with job-products tailored to different market segments. Research in the fast-food industry identifies several employee market segments, including people who work mostly for the money, people whose priority is a consistent work schedule, and people who want to advance and make a career in the industry.[12] Fast-food operators offering one employment package for all are clearly missing the mark.

The growth in the 1980s of such human resource concepts as flexible benefits and flexible work hours ("flexitime") are indicative of the growing heterogeneity of the labor force and the need to be responsive. Rigid thinking is passé. Flexibility is in. Connecticut's Union Trust Bank has been able to hire more mothers of young children as tellers by accommodating their desire not to work when their children are home from school. Dayton-Hudson, the Minneapolis-based retailer, is training thousands of home care providers so its employees can hire qualified babysitters.[13] Marriott Corporation has established a Work and Family Life Department within its human resources function to deal with such issues. Marriott's Vice President of Personnel Services, Kathleen Alexander, says: "If I have 20 housekeepers who quit the same week in June that school lets out to take care of their children, then I have a problem. It doesn't matter if I have a lot of customers if I can't clean the rooms."[14]

Original Research II, a Chicago telephone research company, successfully employs full-time college students to work part-time as interviewers. One factor in its success is allowing the students to redesign their work schedules every two weeks. The company pays bonuses to meet staffing requirements at unpopular times like Saturday.[15] Toys R Us captures employees' locational preferences in its on-line human resources information system, the most sophisticated system of this type we have seen. When the company decided to open stores in Germany, its human resources department immediately provided a list of 42 employees who wanted to work in Germany.[16]

OFFER A VISION

The attraction, development, motivation, and retention of quality employees requires a clear vision worth pursuing. A paycheck may keep a person on the job physically, but it alone will not keep a person on the job emotionally. People delivering service need to know how their work fits in the broader scheme of business operations, how their work contributes to the firm. They need to understand and believe in the goal to which they contribute; they need to have a *cause* because serving others is just too demanding and frustrating to be done well each day without one.

Great internal marketing companies stand for something worthwhile and they communicate this vision to employees with passion. *Passion* is a strange word to use in a business book, but it is the word that best captures the fervent commitment to the goal-oriented values that distinguish the best internal marketing companies from others.

Chick-fil-A, the highly successful Atlanta-based fast-food chain, pursues its vision of product and service integrity with a zeal matched by few competitors. The company is so committed to hands-on, day-to-day management of its more than 400 stores that it insists store operators (independent businesspeople who enter into a partnership with the parent company) run only one store. To attract first-rate operators who could opt for the competition and the possibility of multiple stores, Chick-fil-A splits store profits with the operators on a 50–50 basis.

ServiceMaster's vision is to add dignity to work. Managing janitorial, laundry, and other unglamorous support services for hospitals, schools, and companies, ServiceMaster lives by the principle of "before asking someone to do something you have to help them be something."[17] The Downers Grove, Illinois, company invests in a variety of basic skills training and educational programs to help employees improve their self-image and future prospects. ServiceMaster also emphasizes the contribution each server makes to the end customer. For example, a physician might be asked to address hospital janitorial staff on how a sanitary and neat room improves patients' recovery chances. Chairman and CEO C. William Pollard states: "We have housekeepers relating to their task and saying 'Hey, I've got something to do with that person being well.' . . . [Our people] work better when they understand the value of their contribution."[18]

Visions should be simple, communicated at every opportunity, and communicated personally by top management. Seattle restaurant owner Timothy Firnstahl illustrates the virtues of a simple vision:

I spent considerable time writing Ten Tenets of Excellence for our organization. We included them in our training manuals and posted them in the restaurants and the offices. One day about a year later, someone asked me what the sixth tenet was, and I couldn't tell her. It came to me that if I couldn't remember the Ten Tenets of Excellence, surely no one else could either. That meant the company had no strategy known to its employees.[19]

Stew Leonard's vision is conveyed by the word STEW where S stands for satisfy, T for teamwork, E for excellence, and W for wow. At Deluxe Corporation (formerly Deluxe Check Printers) the vision is error-free printing of bank checks and next-day order shipment. At Southwest Airlines the vision is productivity, fun, and working together as a family.

Smart internal marketers use every opportunity to convey the vision. Delta Airlines considers employees a critical second audience for its advertising and runs campaigns with the dual objectives of reaching the flying public and communicating its vision to employees. Delta frequently uses its own employees in its advertising. Before opening its new headquarters building in Dallas, Southwest Airlines put 11,000 employee photographs on the walls. Russell Vernon, the owner of West Point Market, uses an *Associates Handbook* to help define what the company believes in for all employees.

Senior management's personal involvement in communicating the vision to employees is a must. Bernie Marcus and Arthur Blank, the CEO and president of the home improvement chain, Home Depot, are personally involved in the initial training of store managers. With a plan to grow from 20,000 employees in 1990 to 60,000 in 1995, Marcus and Blank believe their personal involvement is essential to preserving the company's culture.

When British Airways presented more than 400 two-day seminars between 1983 and 1985 to focus employee attention on service improvement, new CEO Sir Colin Marshall was personally involved. "Sir Colin personally opened or closed 70 percent of those classes around the world," says Anthony Lane, managing director of Total Manager International, a human resources development firm in the United Kingdom. "That is extraordinary commitment. But it sends a message that isn't soon forgotten."[20]

PREPARE PEOPLE TO PERFORM

Preparing people to perform and market the service enhances every subgoal of internal marketing: attracting, developing, motivating, and retaining superior employees. Unfortunately, servers are often ill-prepared for the service role. They receive training, but it is too little, or too late, or not the kind of training they need. Or they may receive adequate technical skills training, but they do not receive enough *knowledge;* they learn *how* but not *why.*

A common mistake that companies make is to view employee skills and knowledge development as events (a one-week course, an annual seminar) rather than an ongoing process. The inclination to put employees through a specific training program and then to consider them "trained" is both strong and wrong. Servers need to learn continuously as learning is a confidence builder, a motivating force, and a source of self-esteem. What managers perceive as unmotivated employee behavior is often unconfident employee behavior. Employees are unlikely to be motivated to perform services they do not feel competent and confident to perform. Sometimes managers see employees as unwilling to perform when in fact they are unable to perform.

Middle Managers as Teachers. One of the most positive actions firms can take to improve employee learning is to promote better teachers into middle management. Virtually all employees in large and medium-size organizations report to middle managers to whom they are exposed daily. The opportunity for teaching is great—and often wasted because the wrong people are in charge. They may have been promoted to management positions because they were successful in nonmanagement positions; their service philosophy, their commitment to helping others improve their performance, and their communication skills may not have been considered.

In an earlier book, we discussed two tests that executives could apply in identifying candidates for management positions.[21] Although our focus was identifying people with leadership qualities, the tests are germane, as capacity for teaching is one of the principal characteristics of leaders. The tests are presented in Exhibit 9–3.

Companies need to help existing middle managers become better teachers in addition to improving the selection criteria for new managers. Indeed, managers should take the courses designed for front-line servers before the front-line servers take them. It is demoralizing for employees to return from training and education experiences enthusiastic about applying new skills or knowledge only to confront an insecure supervisor who feels threatened by something new. It is also wasteful because new learning requires repetition and reinforcement to take hold. Just as learning boosts the confidence of front-line servers, so does it boost the confidence (and openness) of the

Exhibit 9–3 Two Tests for Identifying Service Leaders

1. *The footprints-in-the-sand test.* With people, the best predictor of the future is the past. The key is to study a person's past qualitatively, not just quantitatively, and to examine methods, not just outcomes. Some of the questions to ask and answer are:

   - What are the person's greatest career accomplishments — and why?

   - When in positions of authority, what innovations or new directions did this person sponsor?

   - What is this person's philosophy of service? What evidence exists that this individual can be a service champion or service defender?

   - Do signs exist that this person inspires others and builds followership? Do others believe in this individual? Do they believe in his or her integrity?

   - Is there evidence of informal leadership in this person's background, that is, the ability to influence a group without the benefit of an official position or title?

2. *The stand-for-something test.* True leaders are determined pursuers of their vision for the future. They are clear about the direction they wish to go and why. They do not straddle the fence, are not wishy-washy, do not play it safe. As Peter Drucker has written, the leader's first task is to be the trumpet with a clear sound. Thus, a crucial leadership test is the extent to which an individual's beliefs and priorities are on the table, visible for all to see.

Adapted from Valarie A. Zeithaml, A. Parasuraman, and Leonard L. Berry, *Delivering Quality Service: Balancing Customer Perceptions and Expectations* (New York: Free Press, 1990), p. 155.

managers for whom they work. As Berry, Bennett, and Brown write: "Training and education for managers is truly pivotal—for the example it sets, for the understanding it builds, and for the leadership and coaching skills it nurtures."[22]

Health care services consultant Wendy Leebov challenges hospitals to use education to effect mindset changes in middle management. Her list of needed mindset changes, which clearly applies beyond health care, touches the manager-as-teacher issue in every instance:

- From provider orientation to a customer orientation
- From tolerance of status quo to higher standards
- From director to empowerer
- From "employee as replaceable" to "employee as irreplaceable"
- From reactive to proactive
- From tradition and safety to experimentation and risk
- From turf protection to teamwork across lines
- From cynicism to optimism[23]

Becoming a High-Learning Company. A company that makes a strategic commitment to the skill and knowledge development of its employees develops a reputation for investing in people and benefits accordingly. Original Research II offers its employees more than 100 different short workshops or reading packages. Many of these offerings are on subjects requested by the employees, such as using a calculator and memo writing.[24] GTE Mobile Communications unconditionally guarantees employees at least 40 hours of formal classroom education and training annually.[25] Here are some guidelines for making the training and education investment:

1. *Be guided by data.* Use market and employee research data in determining what skills and knowledge to teach. Prepare servers to perform the service their customers expect. Identify the skill and knowledge areas in which servers feel most deficient.

2. *Use a mix of learning approaches.* Use multiple learning approaches, such as classroom instruction, role playing, and self-instructional programming; no single approach fits all needs and people. Be bold and creative. Meridian Banking Group has had employees prepare deposit slips with Vaseline smeared on their glasses and count money with three fingers taped together to help them understand the problems that elderly customers with poor eyesight or arthritis might face in the bank.[26]

3. *Use role models.* Invite the most credible executives to be instructors in company courses. Put them in the position to share their expertise and model their values and style. Also invite successful peers to be instructors and session leaders.

4. *Institutionalize learning.* Devote part of regular staff meetings to skill and knowledge development. Distribute selected articles, videos, or other educational materials systematically. Take employees on field trips to visit other companies and then share with each other the best and worst of what they saw.

5. *Evaluate and fine-tune.* Administer multi-stage evaluations of skill and knowledge development efforts. Find out from employees and their managers what on-the-job changes have resulted from participation in a learning program. Evaluate at several different times after the program has ended, for example, after one and three months.

STRESS TEAM PLAY

Service work is demanding, frequently frustrating, and sometimes demoralizing. The sheer number of customers to serve, such as on a full airline flight or in a busy bank branch at noon on a Friday, can be psychologically and physically overwhelming. Some customers are insensitive if not downright rude. Control over the service is often dispersed among different organizational units that function without cohesion or a unified spirit, limiting contact employees' ability to effectively serve their customers.[27]

It is common for service providers to be so stressed by the service role that they become less caring, less sensitive, less eager to please. What customers perceive as impersonal or bureaucratic behavior is often the coping behavior of weary servers who have endured too many hurts in the real world of service delivery. In effect, the experience of serving becomes a negative.

An Antidote for Burnout. One important dynamic in sustaining servers' motivation to serve is the presence of service "teammates." An interactive community of coworkers who help each other, commiserate, and achieve together is a powerful antidote to service burnout. Team involvement can be rejuvenating, inspirational, and fun. It also raises the stakes for individual performance. Letting down the team may be worse than letting down the boss. Few motivators are more potent than the respect of teammates:

> Deep down, people want to identify with a group, to make a contribution, to express themselves and exercise their creativity. They want to strive together . . . to meet goals. They want to feel good about their jobs, because this translates into feeling good about themselves.[28]

One way teamwork bolsters the will to serve is by enhancing the ability to serve. For servers to come through for their customers, others within the organization must come through for them. Teamwork enhances internal service. Our research shows convincingly that teamwork is central to delivering excellent service. Contact employees in five major service firms who indicate that their organizational units are *not* meeting service standards *disagree* with the following statements:

- I feel that I am part of a team in my unit.
- Everyone in my unit contributes to a team effort in serving customers.
- I feel a sense of responsibility to help my fellow employees do their jobs well.
- My fellow employees and I cooperate more than we compete.
- I feel that I am an important member of this company.[29]

The more people and functions involved in the chain of services leading to the end service, the greater the need for service teams. As University of Southern California's Edward Lawler says: "You have to ask, 'How complex is the work?' The more complex, the more suited it is for teams."[30]

Working at Teamwork. Service team building cannot be left to chance. Internal marketers who think service teams make sense must be prepared to work at teamwork. Sometimes the decisive factor in improved teamwork is an attitude shift of a key player. Bob Legler, President of First Marketing Corporation, a Florida-based producer of customer newsletters, offers the following example:

> For several years, we experienced a continuing strain between our editorial and printing divisions. The constant complaints I heard were "They never give us enough time" from the printing side and, "Why can't they ever do it right" from the editorial folks.
>
> The result was an invisible wall between the two areas and a greater concern for protecting turf than seeing to the client's needs.
>
> Three years ago our printing division director took a new approach. His strategy was to convince his staff (and himself) that our editorial personnel were really his customers and the task of his division was to do whatever it takes to keep the customer happy.
>
> It worked. He has created a culture within the printing division that allows us to meet every delivery no matter how critical the deadline. Morale is at an all time high. And we have a spirit of cooperation far higher than we could have ever imagined.

Attitudinal shifts are usually just part of the answer, however. The richest form of service teamwork requires long-lasting team membership, regular team contact, team leadership, shared goals, and team performance measurement and rewards (in addition to individual employee measurement and rewards). Unfortunately, functional organization structures impede the development of these teamwork characteristics. If the spirit of editorial and printing division teamwork that Bob Legler describes breaks down, he should consider abolishing the two divisions and replacing them with market-based teams. Legler could then assign teams of editorial and printing staff to serve specific accounts. The existing inter-unit structure (printing serving editorial) would become an intra-unit structure (a team of people with different skills serving a common end customer).

Aid Association for Lutherans (AAL) totally reorganized its $50 billion insurance business from a functional structure to a market-team structure in 1987. Before reorganizing, AAL field agents contacted various internal departments for support services, a cumbersome and impersonal process. Field agents now contact an assigned home office team to receive the internal service they need. These all-purpose teams perform more than 150 internal services previously spread throughout the organization. Management gives the restructuring credit for reducing case-processing time by as much as 75 percent.[31]

Aetna Life has reorganized its operations staff into cross-functional teams and has even installed "team" furniture to support the groups. The furniture provides a central work area for team meetings and nearby desks that offer privacy for individual work. Says Aetna executive William Watson, "You don't need to run around the building to get something done."[32]

LEVERAGE THE FREEDOM FACTOR

Human beings were not meant to be robots. Yet managers treat them this way when they use thick policy and procedure manuals to severely limit employees' freedom of action in delivering service. Rule book management undermines employees' confidence in managers, stifles employees' personal growth and creativity, and chases the most able employees out the door in search of more interesting work.

Rule book management usually does not benefit end-customers either. Unempowered employees deliver regimented, "by-the-book" service when a creatively tailored "by-the-customer" service is really needed. While managers rein in servers, customers wish they could be served by "thinking servers."

Two stories surfacing during research for another book demonstrate the virtues of building a culture that encourages service freedom. The first story concerns a banking office manager who kept shivering customers outside on a cold day while he stood inside the door in full view, watch in hand, waiting for opening time to let customers in. When asked why he didn't open early to accommodate the waiting customers, the banker claimed that banking law prevented him from doing so. In fact, it was the bank's policy; law had nothing to do with it.

The second story concerns a distressed bank customer whose ATM card was swallowed by the machine just as she was leaving on a trip. Needing cash for the trip and not near the bank, the customer telephoned a bank officer who sent her the needed $200 in a taxicab.[33]

The two stories illustrate the difference between unthinking and thinking service behaviors. The manager in the first story is nothing more than an enforcer of rules; and the officer in the second story, it turns out, ignored bank policy by sending the money by cab. Although his actions cost little money and helped a desperate customer (who now raves about the bank's fantastic service), the banker probably would have been turned down had he asked his superior, according to the bank's executive vice president. Nonetheless, thinking behavior prevailed and the customer, banker, and bank benefited. Often, however, unthinking behavior prevails and customer, server, and company all lose out.

Service companies do need rules, of course. Airline travelers certainly want pilots to follow the rules of flight safety. We are not advocating the elimination of policies and procedures; what we are advocating is thinning the rule book to its bare essentials. Good internal marketing involves giving servers the opportunity to create for their customers and achieve for themselves. As Lowell Mayone, Vice President of Personnel and Services for Hallmark Cards, puts it: "Empowerment gives people the best avenue to succeed and gives them ownership of the success."[34]

Practicing the other facets of internal marketing discussed in this chapter encourages empowerment. Executives have the confidence to award authority and responsibility—which is what empowerment means—when they truly compete for talent. A strong, well-defined vision guides employee behavior and fewer rules are needed. Skill and knowledge development gives employees the confidence to innovate for customers. The interdependencies and shared goals of team play stimulate individual initiative.

Empowering employees is not easy. Some employees would prefer everything spelled out so they would not have the additional pressure of creative problem-solving and the risk of making errors in judgment. It is, after all, less work and less risky to tell a custo*r* nothing can be done than to send the customer $200 in a t*a* will managers necessarily welcome more authority for th*e* reports—and less control for themselves.

Pushing authority and responsibility downward into the *o*

tion, close to the customer, requires determination, patience, and conscious efforts to thin the rule book. Most service companies would benefit from task forces that review existing policies and procedures with the mandate to modify or discard those that unnecessarily restrict service freedom. Companies would also benefit from training and education programs that teach front-line servers values, not just rules. And performance measurement and reward systems need to encourage creativity and initiative on behalf of customers.

Moreover, firms need to directly address the issue of empowerment in educating and training managers. Managers must be taught and retaught the dangers of overmanagement; they must learn about the good that can come from widening the solution boundaries for their people.

MEASURE AND REWARD

The goals of internal marketing are thwarted if employee performance is not measured and rewarded. People at work need to know that they will be measured on how well they do and that it is worthwhile to do well. Job-products that offer the opportunity for achievement are most likely to fit the needs of human beings, yet achievement remains unidentified and uncelebrated without measurement and rewards.

Unfortunately, many service companies do a poor job of building an achievement culture. Performance measurement systems often focus exclusively on *output measures,* such as size or accuracy of transactions, and ignore *behavioral measures,* such as customer perception of the responsiveness or empathy of the service. Moreover, performance feedback to employees may be infrequent or not presented constructively. Sometimes measurement leads to no apparent consequence; the employees who perform well fare no better than others in compensation, advancement, or recognition.

Firms intent on rewarding the best performers often focus too narrowly on financial incentives and do not reap the benefits of multiple forms of recognition. Dallas consultant George Rieder studied the relative importance of different rewards to commercial and corporate account managers in a large North American bank. Rieder found that they considered responsibility and authority, a personalized development plan, and sales skills training to be among the most important. Dollars were important but not all-important.[35]

A Few Guidelines on Measurement. The key to an effective reward system is an effective performance measurement system that identifies who deserves the rewards. An effective system measures performance that most contributes to the company's vision and strategy, and it does so in a clear, timely, and fair manner. Convoluted or complicated systems fail to focus employee attention—one of the principal objectives of performance measurement. Infrequent feedback does not provide the regular reinforcement that the objectives of teaching and continual improvement require. Reviewing a series of studies on the application of behavioral management techniques in service companies, Luthans and Davis write:

> As most of the studies showed, the feedback of service performance information to employees can be a powerful intervention strategy for behavioral management. In a surprisingly large number of cases, service employees have little idea of how they are doing. Regularly displayed feedback can keep employees aware of their performance and, as shown in the studies reviewed, lead them to increase desirable service behaviors.[36]

Unfair systems undermine the credibility of the measurement feedback they produce and the reward decisions they influence. Characteristics of a fair performance measurement system are enumerated in Exhibit 9–4.

Performance measurement and reward systems symbolize a company's culture in a powerful way. Employees know that management measures and rewards what is important. Thus, it is beneficial to disseminate performance measurement data to the appropriate senior executives. People in the trenches of service organizations performing work that at least some of the time is intrinsically unrewarding need to know that significant others in the organization will be aware of their performance.

A Few Guidelines on Rewards. Here are several reward-system guidelines developed from our studies of service organizations and interviews with service employees:

- Link rewards to the firm's vision and strategy. Reward performance that moves the firm in the intended direction.
- Distinguish between competence pay (compensation for doing one's job) and performance pay (extra rewards for outstanding performance).
- Use multiple methods to reward outstanding performers, includ-

Exhibit 9–4 Characteristics of a Fair Performance Measurement System

---

• The measures relate directly to service standards. There is consistency between the priorities of a service role and the manner in which role performance is measured.

• Service providers are prepared to perform the service role. They have been given the opportunity to learn the skills and knowledge they need to do well in the measurement system.

• Service providers have provided input on the appropriateness and fairness of the measures that are used.

• The measurement approaches have been explained to those whose performance is being measured.

• The measures are administered on an ongoing basis to minimize the impact of a single measurement encounter.

• The measures are as uniform as possible among work groups so that everyone plays by the same rules.

• Multiple measures are used to overcome the disadvantages of any one approach and to provide different-angled views of service performance.

Adapted from Leonard L. Berry, David R. Bennett, and Carter W. Brown, *Service Quality—A Profit Strategy for Financial Institutions* (Homewood, Ill.: Dow Jones-Irwin, 1989), p. 176.

ing financial rewards, nonfinancial recognition, and career advancement. Consider the possibilities of rewarding employees with stock and making them owners.

• Remember the power of a pat on the back. Rewards need not always be elaborate or expensive; the sincerity of the recognition is most important.

• Compete for the sustained commitment of employees. Develop enduring reward systems and use short-term programs such as sales contests sparingly or not at all.

• Stress the positive. Use reward systems to celebrate achievement rather than to punish.

• Give everyone a chance. Avoid the trap of rewarding people in some positions (for example, field salespeople) but not in other positions (for example, secretaries). Remember that *all* employees perform some kind of service for someone, their performance can be measured and they need the opportunity to excel and be recognized.

- Reward teams and not just individuals. Reinforce team play with team rewards, while also rewarding superior individual performers.

All but the smallest organizations have three groups of employees: those who, for whatever reason, are not performing well; those who are performing competently but not exceptionally; and those who are outstanding. Effectively measuring and rewarding employee performance affects all three groups. Some members of the bottom group either leave or improve. Members of the middle group have reason to strive for improvement. And members of the top group are less likely to feel unappreciated and leave. Alexander "Sandy" Berry, Senior Executive Vice President of Signet Bank in Richmond, Virginia, states: "Words alone won't work. What is measured and rewarded, recognized or promoted will work."

KNOW THY CUSTOMER

Marketing's oldest axiom is to know the customer. Satisfying customers requires that decision-makers first understand their wants and needs. Employees are customers too, buying job-products from their employers. Designing job-products that attract, develop, motivate, and retain these internal customers demands sensitivity to their aspirations, attitudes, and concerns. Assumptions about what employees want and feel often are wrong, and practicing the art of marketing research is as important in internal marketing as in external marketing.

Linda Cooper, Vice President of Consumer Affairs at First Chicago, describes a situation in her bank where mystery shopping scores for tellers were consistently low on the item "willingness to help." This was a real problem because the bank's analysis of what factor most influences customers to recommend the bank to a friend showed it was "willingness to help." Another bank executive thought that more training was the answer. Cooper was not so sure and held several discussions with groups of tellers. What she learned was that the tellers were upset at their supervisors and the bank. One significant issue was that tellers were closely instructed about which transactions were acceptable and which were not, e.g., exceeding check-cashing limits. However, if customers complained, supervisors sometimes overrode the tellers—with tellers losing face in front of customers. Cooper's remedy was to have the tellers and supervisors jointly agree on a written guideline for overrides. (In this case, adding to the rulebook made sense.)

This story illustrates the need to listen to service performers in service businesses. The bank used research with end-customers to learn that it had a problem. Had it relied on the one executive's assumption about the solution to the problem and not made the effort to listen to the tellers, it probably would have wasted considerable time and money on the wrong solution.

First Chicago is an ardent practitioner of employee research. In addition to holding monthly focus group interviews with employee groups, the bank has installed an employee telephone hot line called "2-Talk" that is answered in the Consumer Affairs Department's Action Center. Employees are encouraged to call 2-Talk whenever they receive poor service themselves, witness service problems, or have service-improvement ideas.

Each quarter retail bank employees receive a questionnaire to which they respond anonymously. The questionnaire is accompanied by a letter from the banking group head summarizing the findings from the previous survey and the actions taken. In a recent year the first quarter's survey included questions such as: "Do you have what you need to do your job?" and "Does the equipment work?" The second quarter survey concerned employees' attitudes toward the bank's services, prices, and communications. The third quarter survey focused on employees' perceptions of internal service quality. The fourth quarter survey covered employees' satisfaction with their immediate supervisors and senior management. Employees rated managers on issues such as whether they discussed work priorities, appreciated extra effort, and were visible. The following questions also were asked:

- Would you refer a friend to work here?
- Would you bank here if you weren't an employee?
- If you were president of the bank, what changes would you make to improve service quality and morale?[37]

Internal marketing research backfires unless management is prepared to take action on significant findings. The *New York Times* cites an unidentified company that learned of employee unhappiness with the company's cafeteria from an employee survey. Management reported the survey results in the employee newsletter and then did nothing to improve the cafeteria. One manager says: "Before we could kid ourselves that the bosses did not know how bad the cafeteria was. After the survey, we knew they just didn't care."[38] First Pennsylvania Bank Vice Chairman Les Butler states: "Don't ask if you really don't want to hear. Don't ask if you only seek your preconceived answer. Value the input, value the participation, explain why their ideas are being sought and how they will be used."

SUMMARY AND ACTION CHECKLIST

A service company can be only as good as its people. A service is a performance, and it is usually difficult to separate the performance from the people. If the people don't meet customers' expectations, then neither does the service. Investing in people quality in a service business means investing in product quality.

To realize its potential in services marketing, a firm must realize its potential in internal marketing—the attraction, development, motivation, and retention of qualified employee-customers through need-meeting job-products. Internal marketing paves the way for external marketing of services.

The companies that practice internal marketing most effectively will (1) compete aggressively for talent market share; (2) offer a vision that brings purpose and meaning to the workplace; (3) equip people with the skills and knowledge to perform their service roles excellently; (4) bring people together to benefit from the fruits of team play; (5) leverage the freedom factor; (6) nurture achievement through measurement and rewards; and (7) base job-product design decisions on research.

These seven components of internal marketing practice lend themselves to the following action checklist:

1. *Do we compete as hard for employees as we do for end-customers?* Are we imaginative in how we compete for talent? Are we bold? Do we experiment and try new strategies? Do we use a variety of media? Do we use the right people to recruit and interview? People who will make a strong impression? People who can sell?

2. *Does our company stand for something worthwhile?* Do we offer our employees a vision that they can grab hold of and believe in? Do we have a reason for being that makes our company a special place to work? Do we communicate our

vision well? Do we weave it into our company culture at every opportunity?

3. *Do we prepare our people to perform excellently?* Do we view skill and knowledge development as an investment rather than an expense? Do we view it as an ongoing process rather than as an event? Do we view it as a confidence builder and a motivator? Do we teach our people "why" and not just "how?" Do we go beyond training and educate as well?

4. *Do we stress team play?* Does our organizational structure foster teamwork? Do our physical work environments? Do our training and educational efforts? Do our performance measurement and reward systems? Do our employees understand where they fit in the company team? Do they understand the big picture?

5. *Do we allow our employees the freedom to come through for their customers?* Do we make rules that fit the aspirations of our best employees rather than protect us from our worst employees? Do we work at keeping our policy and procedure manuals thin? Do we work at building empowerment into our culture?

6. *Do we measure and reward that which is important?* Do we measure and reward employee performance that contributes most to our vision? Do we use multiple methods to measure and to reward? Do we emphasize fairness in the methods we use? Do we give all employees the opportunity to be recognized for their excellence?

7. *Do we listen to our employees?* Do we use formal and informal research techniques to investigate their attitudes, concerns, and needs? Do we proactively solicit their input? Do we act on what we learn? Do we use the data to improve the job-product?

PART

V

Peering Ahead

10

❖❖❖

Services Marketing in the Nineties

We have written this book to convey the services marketing perspective and the central role of quality in services marketing. The pursuit of superior service performance will shape the evolution of services marketing in the 1990s. No other force will be as influential and pervasive. We finish our book by reflecting on how services marketing will change in the 1990s. Before peering into the future, however, we briefly summarize this book's primary themes.

THE QUALITY IMPERATIVE

Service quality is the foundation for services marketing. High quality service gives credibility to the field sales force and the advertising, stimulates favorable word-of-mouth communications, enhances customers' perception of value, and boosts the morale and loyalty of employees and customers alike. Service quality is not a separate discipline from services marketing; service quality is the central part *of* services marketing. Companies with poor service cannot succeed in marketing no matter how enticing their advertising or how many calls their salespeople make. Advertising and sales entreaties only persuade more people to experience a poor service and learn firsthand to avoid the firm in the future.

The core of service quality is reliability—keeping the service promise. Firms that routinely break their promises, that are not dependable, that make frequent mistakes, lose the confidence of their customers. And the confidence of customers is a service firm's most precious asset.

Friendliness does not compensate for broken service promises. Hotel customers expect their guaranteed reservations to be honored; bank customers expect their monthly bank statements to be correct; dry-cleaning customers expect their shirt collars to be folded properly every time. Most customers appreciate a sincere apology when the service promise is broken, but the apology does not erase the memory of an unreliable service. If a pattern of failure develops, customers conclude the firm cannot be counted on, friendly or not.

Excellent recovery service is critical to bolster customer confidence in the firm's *service values*. Recovery cannot change the reality of an initial service failure, but it can demonstrate a firm's ambition to serve well and position the initial failure as an aberration. The stakes are high because ineffective recovery means disappointing the customer twice—with the initial service and then again with the recovery service. Our data show that such a "double deviation"[1] from customers' expectations significantly undermines their confidence in the firm's service.

Service firms must be reliable just to compete. They must be more than reliable to create such a strong impression that customers abandon competitors. Firms are supposed to do what they promise to do. Thus, service failures receive more attention than successes. The best opportunity to demonstrate excellent service is during the service process when provider and customer interact. During the service process, it is possible to *surprise* customers. Service firms need to surprise customers to exceed their expectations, and they occasionally need to exceed customers' expectations to develop a reputation for superior service.

SERVICES MARKETING IS DIFFERENT

The central role of service quality in marketing effectiveness and the inseparability of production and consumption for many services make services marketing an "in-the-field" discipline. It is in the stores and branch offices and over the telephone that services are sold or not, delivered as promised or not, performed with inspiration or without. The best services marketing directors focus their energies not on performing marketing for the firm, but on inducing the firm to perform marketing; they focus their energies on developing human potential for serving and selling. Outstanding services marketing directors understand Quinn and Paquette's description of service companies as "voluntary organizations," and they invest in creating an environment in which servers want to perform well and are able to perform well.[2]

Marketing a performance is not the same as marketing an object. Services marketing is especially different from packaged goods marketing as shown in Exhibit 1–3 in the first chapter. Many marketing executives joining service organizations from packaged goods backgrounds have learned the hard way that services marketing is different. In packaged goods the emphasis is on differentiating tangibles through imagery; in services the emphasis is tangibilizing the intangible. In packaged goods the emphasis is on branding individual products; in services it is on branding the company. In packaged goods, marketing managers "push" product to the trade and "pull" consumers through advertising; in services, managers market to employees so that they will sell and perform the service for end-customers. In packaged goods, marketers seek brand loyalty primarily through nonpersonalized means; in services, the goal is relationships, and tailored, personalized contact is a primary tool.

Services marketers segment, position, price, and promote just as packaged goods marketers do. Many of the tasks in services and packaged goods marketing are described by the same words; what differ are the perspectives required to be successful in services marketing. The performers are the product, and there is nothing to fall back on if the performance is sub-par.

Four perspectives will greatly influence the development of services marketing in the 1990s:

- The extended corporation
- Thinking big, but acting small
- Friendly computers
- Raised service aspirations and quality habits

THE EXTENDED CORPORATION

In the 1990s, corporate ethnocentrism will increasingly give way to corporate collaboration in the service sector. The concept of the corporation as one entity, fortress-like and independent, will decline and the concept of corporate partnering will rise. Increasingly, service companies will concentrate on what they do best and align with other companies having something valuable to offer that is integral to their service.

The extended corporation concept has been developing most quickly in manufacturing. For example, a growing number of manufacturers are seeking to improve product quality and productivity by working more collaboratively with fewer vendors. Xerox reduced its suppliers from 5,000 to 500 to work more closely with suppliers on just-in-time inventory management and quality improvement. Suppliers now attend Xerox's in-house course on quality. When David Luther, Corporate Director of Quality at Corning, keynoted the 1990 Conference Board Quality Conference he brought with him a customer, a supplier, a union leader, and even a local elementary school principal. They spoke individually about why and how they are working in partnership with Corning more than in the past. Union chief Larry Bankowski stated: "Why is the union involved in total quality? The answer is 'survival.' We cannot survive in the global market with mediocre quality."[3]

More service company alignments will develop for the same basic reason that manufacturer-sponsored alliances are developing: pooling resources and working cooperatively can enhance quality and lower costs. Just as teamwork inside the corporation can boost quality and productivity, so can teamwork outside the corporation. Transforming outsiders to insiders is the central tenet of the extended corporation.

Several years ago, senior executives from Procter & Gamble and Wal-Mart met for two days to explore how they could jointly apply quality management principles to the disposable diaper business. As a result of this meeting, a team of Procter & Gamble employees moved to Bentonville, Arkansas, Wal-Mart's headquarters, to work with Wal-Mart executives on productivity and quality issues. Wal-Mart has increased its Procter & Gamble diaper business by 50 percent and cut inventory time by 70 percent because of this collaboration.[4]

AMRIS, a subsidiary of American Airlines' parent company AMR Corporation, formed a joint venture with Marriott, Hilton, and Budget Rent-A-Car to develop and market a computerized-reservation and yield-management system for the hotel and rental car industries.[5] AMRIS brings to the table its considerable experience and expertise from developing the SABRE travel reservation and information system; from its partners it seeks cost-sharing as well as hotel and rental-car industry expertise and credibility.

The P&G/Wal-Mart liaison and the AMRIS/Marriott/Hilton/Budget Rent-A-Car joint venture illustrate a significant point about extending the corporation: strategic alliances can be anything their partners want them to be so long as they are ethical and lawful. We expect to see more service companies collaborate on functions such as training and marketing research, for example. Consider the possibility of a bank, supermarket chain, and department store chain forming a sales and service training company that conducts in-house programs and markets programs on the outside. By pooling their resources, the three firms may lower internal training costs, generate extra cash flow, and, most importantly, improve the level and extent of training. The principles of excellent selling and service are not industry or company-specific; differences are more habitual perception than actualities.

Extending the corporation is not without pitfalls, of course. Seeking partners with common corporate values and needs, beginning with small projects, devoting ample time to planning, and creating a structure that fosters ongoing communication and teamwork are a few keys to overcoming the risks.

THINK BIG, ACT SMALL

THINKING BIG

The best managed service firms in the 1990s will think big but act small. Thinking big is one part global outlook, one part boundaryless learning, and one part forward motion. Globalization affects every service firm, regardless of whether a firm's management intends to compete abroad. In reality, the free flow of goods, services, and ideas throughout the world influences customers' expectations, tastes, and options as never before. Furniture stores in Philadelphia are affected by IKEA's entry into the market and its popularization of Scandinavian-design, self-assembly furniture. America's domestic airlines are affected by the high service levels of foreign carriers such as Singapore Airlines and SAS. The local furrier is affected by France's Galeries Lafayette advertising an international 800 telephone number to sell "faux furs" in America.[6]

Smart American executives will travel extensively abroad in search of new ideas, new insight into foreign cultures, new opportunities. They will join study missions to foreign countries; read widely about global markets, trends, and competition; and identify counterparts abroad with whom they can be in regular contact. And they will consider the option of growth outside the United States far more readily than heretofore.

A global outlook nurtures competitiveness. It took Toys R Us 35 years to gain 10 percent of the U.S. toy market but just three years to gain 10 percent market share in the United Kingdom. As we complete this book, Toys R Us is seeking to enter Japan in joint venture with McDonald's, despite massive political resistance by Japanese toy retailers. Moto Photo, a one-hour photo processing firm in Dayton, Ohio, has successfully expanded its quick-service system to Canada, Sweden, and Norway, with impressive results.[7]

One way that firms improve their competitiveness is through boundaryless learning, the conscious seeking of knowledge outside familiar, conventional boundaries. Executives who search for cross-cultural knowledge exhibit one kind of boundaryless learning. Executives who read and attend conferences outside their industry exhibit another form of boundaryless learning. Boundaryless learning requires conscious effort. Fred Smith, the founder and chairman of Federal Express, reads about four hours a day from a wide variety of sources. In an interview with *Inc. Magazine*, he discussed how his interdisciplinary reading helped the company:

> It became obvious that we had to track at every moment every item that was given to us. And when we got to thinking about it, it looked as if it was impossible. . . . At the time, I had been reading some very different types of things about the grocery business and the price performance of computers.
>
> Well, one thing led to another, and we began to look into using a version of those bar codes that are on the soup cans to give a number in sequence to every package. It turned out to be a good idea. . . . Without it, we could not have controlled this organization.[8]

Thinking big is also forward motion, the commitment to build the new and renew the old. Big thinkers cannot stand still and still be big thinkers. Thus, Federal Express buys Tiger International and takes some early losses to position itself as a global player; Disney develops EPCOT Center, becomes a major hotel company, revitalizes its movie business with the Touchstone label, opens a movie-industry theme park, and goes international; and in 1991 Stew Leonard's opens its second store, a 137,000 square-foot megastore in Danbury, Connecticut, just 17 miles from the flagship store in Norwalk.

ACTING SMALL

Acting small is as important as thinking big. Acting small is the opposite of acting bureaucratically. Carolyn Burstein of the Federal Quality Institute notes four characteristics of bureaucracies:[9]

- Management by rules
- Functional organization structure
- An inward focus
- Purposely treating customers impersonally

Acting small, in contrast, means a thin rulebook, a seamless organizational structure that fosters quick response, an external focus on customer needs, and purposely treating customers personally. It means capitalizing on the opportunity to interact with end-customers by delivering a creative, sincere, personal service. Acting small does *not* mean contrived or programmed personalization. Indeed, research by Surprenant and Solomon shows that canned personalization reduces customers' confidence in employees' ability.[10]

Acting small is not an automatic result of being small; it is, like thinking big, more a function of leadership. There are small, bureaucratic companies and large, responsive companies. Stew Leonard's may have 100,000 customers visit its Norwalk store in a week, but it excels at making each one of them feel important. American Express has invested millions of dollars in technology, systems, and training to develop the capability to resolve immediately 85 percent of the problems that prompt card holders to call the 800 number listed on their monthly statement.

It is easier, of course, for a small company to act small than a big company—and well-managed small firms leverage this advantage in competing against large firms. Dial-a-Mattres, a New York City firm, guarantees delivery of a new mattress within two hours of receiving the order or it cuts the price by 10 percent. One customer flying on the Concorde from Paris phoned Dial-a-Mattres while over the Atlantic and ordered a mattress for her Manhattan apartment. It was waiting for her when she arrived.[11]

Direct Tire Sales, a successful one-store tire and automotive service company near Boston, is another company that acts small. To respond to apartment dwellers' problems of finding storage space for snow tires in the warm months and regular tires during the winter, Direct Tire rented a trailer and started a tire storage service. The company stores the tires and mounts and balances them twice a year for a $100 annual fee. Direct Tire also uses loaner cars extensively because that is what many customers want when they give up their own car for service. President Barry Steinberg explains:

> Three years ago, before I had the loaners, I was doing $50,000 to $55,000 a month in service work. Today I'm averaging $120,000 a month, and the gross margins on service work are 30 percent higher than on tires. People will call up and say, "I understand you have a free car I can use while you work on mine." We'll say, "Yes, that's right," and they'll schedule an appointment right then. A lot of them don't even bother to ask what the work will cost. I'm going to add more cars.[12]

FRIENDLY COMPUTERS

A primary means to acting small is the computer. Depersonalized, bureaucratic service failures frequently attributed to computers by service employees and customers often are a function of the way computers are used, not a function of computerization itself. Computers can be service employees' and customers' best friend. Computers can lessen mundane and boring work, personalize information, save time, and enfeeble bureaucracy.

Computers can be a tireless servant when used to support a clear strategy. Computers are a tool, a means to an end. Smart managers use computers to meet the needs of internal and/or external customers. They learn the requirements, preferences, work styles or lifestyles, and technical literacy of targeted groups and then design computer systems that are as natural and responsive to customer needs as possible. And they back up the technology with human support.

The best-managed service firms in the 1990s will be high-tech *and* high-touch, not one or the other. They will use computers to support people delivering service and to add value to services; and they will use people to back up the computers when something goes awry and to accomplish objectives that computers can't, such as nurturing personalized client relationships.

Marshaling the power of friendly computers is a human process. Dylex Ltd., a Toronto-based retail clothing chain, temporarily assigned its information systems manager to manage one of its stores to experience directly the realities of store operations. From this experience, the information manager was able to design a simple data entry system that significantly improved inventory management.[13] Putting the information manager into the role of store manager fostered a user-focus that is often missing in computer system design.

MULTIPLYING KNOWLEDGE

Service executives increasingly will turn to friendly computers to multiply knowledge. Whereas service providers unaided by databases are limited to their own knowledge, those who can access well-conceived information systems effectively possess the knowledge of many. And because knowledge is power, multiplying the knowledge of front-line servers can have the beneficial effects of minimizing bureaucracy and leveraging service freedom.[14] If servers have the knowledge they need to serve, why muddle the process with unnecessary steps and authorizations?

The SABRE reservation and information system—described by one of its developers as an "electronic travel supermarket"—now operates in more than 14,500 subscriber locations in more than 40 countries. SABRE and competitive systems have decentralized and simplified travel reservations and ticket distribution. Travel agents now sell more than 80 percent of all passenger tickets compared to less than 40 percent in 1976.[15] Travel agencies would have been unable to function in an industry characterized by millions of fare changes each month without these broad-based knowledge systems.

Friendly computers also can multiply end-customers' knowledge. The Central Hardware home center chain has installed an interactive video information system in each of its stores. Among other services, the system offers do-it-yourself video segments featuring step-by-step instructions for 19 home-improvement projects. Customers can touch the screen to obtain a printout listing the steps needed to complete the project.[16]

STREAMLINING SERVICE

Friendly computers can streamline services by eliminating or automating manual functions. Melding machine and human energy can quicken service delivery and improve service accessibility. It can free servers from boring, repetitive functions better performed by computers, thus improving the productivity of routine service delivery and allowing a broader menu of personal services.

Chemical Bank has developed a PC-based retail banking system

Genesys that serves each employee group having direct contact with customers. One result of Genesys is a capability through automated credit scoring to make personal loan decisions (and even cut the check) in five minutes.

Progressive Casualty Insurance Company in Cleveland has implemented a hybrid system that allows telephone switches and computers to communicate. Telephoning clients enter their account numbers on touch-tone phones, producing a display of their records on service representatives' computer screens as soon as they answer the call. If the call is transferred, the files appear on the screen of the representative taking the transferred call.[17]

The Aurora, Colorado, police department is one of several police departments in the country that has computerized its 911 emergency service to such a degree that the caller's telephone number and address is displayed on the operator's screen within one second after answering. By punching one button, the operator can display any recent police calls to that address; another button displays the closest patrol cars. With the Aurora police department receiving 190,000 such calls in 1990 (and with New York City's 911 lines ringing every seven seconds), information technology is the only way to free "prisoners of 911" for imaginative crime prevention.[18]

Hyatt Hotels is testing the use of magnetic card readers on the door locks of guest rooms. The card reader can communicate with the hotel's computer. Guests are told their room number when making reservations, and they are advised to proceed directly to the room, entering by putting their credit card through the magnetic reader. The hotel operator knows the guest has arrived, and message-taking and billing commence once the card is put through the reader. Hyatt's marketing director, Adam Aron, states: "Our corporate objective is to eliminate the front desk in our hotels."[19]

CUSTOMIZING SERVICE

Services marketing in the 1990s will not only be characterized by high-tech *and* high-touch strategy but also by high touch *through* high-tech strategy. Computer-based systems that distribute the right information on individual customers (or their possessions) to the right service provider at the right time provide an opportunity to custom-fit the service cost-effectively. Information technology is the principal weapon in forging the level three relationship marketing strategies discussed in Chapter 8. Tom Regnier, Managing Director of Marketing Research, Business Incentives Inc., states:

> Technology will allow larger service companies to offer customers a seamless experience even though service representatives will have literally millions of records at their fingertips. It will enable companies to offer their customers the hands-on personal service that once was the key to successful service quality operations provided by service entrepreneurs.

USAA Insurance Company is using optical scanning technology to store and retrieve client correspondence. When a client telephones the company the representative is able to say "Yes, Colonel Smith, I have your letter in front of me."

Walgreen, a Chicago-based chain of more than 1,600 drugstores, uses a system of satellite dishes and a computerized database to provide its pharmacists in 29 states instant access to customers' prescription records regardless of where prescriptions were first filled. Thus, a Walgreen customer living in Texas can refill a prescription while traveling in Arizona.[20] Customers can request a printout of their Walgreen prescription purchases for tax and insurance records.

Xerox has introduced copier products with sensors to detect a developing operating problem; a modem notifies a central computer at Xerox. If the central computer determines that standards are not being met, it telephones the Xerox repair service closest to the malfunctioning machine, which then telephones the customer to make an appointment.[21] Wayne Light, manager of Xerox's customer service strategy office, states:

> Nine of 10 times [when] a customer has an interaction with Xerox, it's because a machine is down and we have to send a technician into a hostile environment. Now if a threshold is exceeded—if the timing of paper moving through the system is off, for example—that information is sent back to an expert system which evaluates the problem, and electronically communicates to our work support dispatch team that within 24 to 48 hours they will have a problem with that machine. Our goal is to have 50 percent of customer interactions with Xerox involve a technician coming out to fix a problem *before* a customer knows it's there.[22]

RAISED ASPIRATIONS AND QUALITY HABITS

The process of improving quality is difficult to begin and to sustain. Quality-improvement rhetoric is widespread; substantive change is more difficult to find. Progressive companies exist in every industry, but most companies are still in the "talking-about-quality" stage rather than their "cultural-change" stage. Many observers of the service quality scene in America are skeptical. One skeptic told us:

> While we are currently undergoing a rebirth of service quality emphasis, I don't anticipate that a majority of firms will make inroads into improvement. It is just too much of a commitment for them. I equate the service quality improvement process to going on a diet. There are lots of diet books. In fact there are probably more books on diet than on any subject other than money. At any one time, about 25 percent of American adults are on a diet, yet we are not wasting away as a people. There will have to be fundamental change, perhaps initiated by crisis, before American companies will change.

We believe the 1990s can be a decade of genuine progress in service quality in America, in part because the crisis our skeptical friend mentions already exists in most service industries—from department store retailing to airlines, from network television broadcasting to banking. Global, Darwinian competition will characterize virtually every major service industry in this decade; there will be ample crisis to go around. An already strong stimulus for change—global competition—will become even more forceful in the years immediately ahead.

The "talking-about-quality" stage still underway will abet the change process. With talking comes some listening, and with some listening comes some learning. American executives are more aware today than 10 years ago that service quality is important to customers; that it is the basis for competitive differentiation, the cornerstone of relationship marketing, the best way to compete on value rather than price, and a key to internal marketing (just as internal marketing is a key to service quality).

Transforming talk into action is no sure thing, of course. Crisis provides the incentive and learning brings awareness of new possibilities, but individuals throughout an organization still need to assume the mantle of service leadership and do something. A thought and action revolution on two levels is needed.

The first level concerns our aspirations. It is time in America to raise our service standards, to extend our ambitions, to aspire to be the best servers in the world. Americans have long aspired to be world-class in other venues; the stakes are high to become similarly ambitious in the delivery of service. Ten essential attitude shifts for improving service quality are enumerated in Exhibit 10–1.

On the second level, executives must learn how to integrate service improvement into the organization, how to make it a habit, how to weave it into the fabric of company culture. Striving for service excellence needs to be *expected* operating procedure rather than *elective* operating procedure. Here are five steps companies can take to make service improvement a habit.

1. *Build a service quality information system.* Service quality research is most likely to influence decision-making when performed in multiple ways on an ongoing basis and when its results are systematically shared with and discussed by executives. A service quality study is not enough; companies need to build information systems that executives use regularly in making decisions.[23] The type and fre-

From	To
Being good	Being excellent
Quality of products	Quality in everything
Management support	Management involvement
Functional isolationism	Team energy
Quality is someone else's concern	Quality is my concern
Some employees have customers	All employees have customers
Recovery as a problem	Recovery as an opportunity
Errors are inevitable	Doing it right every time
Service is shapeless	Service-system design
Quality-improvement programs	Continuous improvement

Exhibit *10–1* Ten Essential Attitude Shifts for Improving Service Quality

quency of research that might form the foundation of a service quality information system are listed in Exhibit 10-2.

2. *Report key service statistics.* Disclosing key quality statistics publicly and at the highest corporate levels helps stimulate and sustain internal interest in quality. Deluxe Corporation discloses in its annual report the percentage of orders that it prints without error and ships by its next-day standard. Quality performance is the first agenda item at Corning board meetings. A growing number of firms now require operating unit heads to report on quality performance during reviews with top management.

3. *Measure the profit impact of poor quality.* Companies need to formally measure the cost of poor quality and incorporate these data into the analysis of a business unit's profit contribution. For example, firms can compute average costs for reperforming botched services and multiply by the frequency of occurrence to derive service rework costs. Firms can estimate from research the percentage of customers who defect for service-related reasons, calculate the annual profit contribution of different types of customers, and then calculate lost profit caused by service failures. Executives whose per-

Type of Research	Frequency
Customer complaint solicitation	Continuous
Post-transaction follow-up surveys	Continuous
Managers telephoning customers for informal feedback	Weekly
Customer focus groups	Monthly
"Mystery shopping" of service providers	Quarterly
Employee surveys	Quarterly
Total market service quality surveys	3 times/year
Special purpose research	As needed

Exhibit *10-2* Building a Service Quality Information System

SOURCE: A. Parasuraman, Leonard L. Berry, and Valarie A. Zeithaml, "Guidelines for Conducting Service Quality Research," *Marketing Research,* December 1990, p. 43.

formance is measured and rewarded on the basis of profit contribution will become more interested in quality.

4. *Stress personal quality.* Senior managers should use every opportunity to stress the personal responsibility of each employee for quality improvement. All employees should have the opportunity to participate on quality-improvement teams on company time. All employees should be encouraged to submit quality-improvement suggestions. All employees should attend a quality-improvement course within their first few months on the job. All employees should devote a predetermined percentage of total work time to training and education each year. All employees should be evaluated on their contribution to quality improvement as part of their formal performance appraisals.

5. *Showcase service leadership.* Companies seeking the Malcolm Baldrige Quality Award benefit because the process of applying offers a framework for thinking about quality, identifies weaknesses, and energizes the organization. Even though only a few companies can win the award each year the organizational self-evaluation creates a quality progress profile.

Medium-sized and larger companies should start in-house quality awards programs in addition to participating in the Baldrige program. Well-managed in-house programs can offer many of the same benefits as the Baldrige, plus an important extra benefit: one or more units win in each company. Having winners to shower with praise and tribute in the presence of peers showcases service leadership. Winning units set the tone for others in the organization and raise their own self-expectations. They become lighthouses for change, helping to sustain the culture-change process.

IN CLOSING

The spirit of this book is the elegant simplicity of services marketing. Services marketing is more fundamentals than fanciness, more common sense than hard science, more perspiration than promotion. Services marketing is execution, not just strategy; inspiration, not just mechanics; promise-keeping, not just promise-making.

The great service companies strongly execute a strong service concept; they do the little things better than their competitors; they effectively manage the clues of the business; they listen carefully to employees and to customers; they invest in the performers of the service; they strive to exceed customers' expectations, to "wow" customers; they take excellent care of existing customers; and they always try to improve their service performance.

The essence of services marketing is service. When the product is a performance, nothing is more important than performance quality.

Notes

Chapter 1
Services and Quality

1. The first two stories are adapted from Leonard L. Berry, "In Services, Little Things Make the Big Stories," *American Banker,* April 28, 1988, p. 4; the third story is adapted from Leonard L. Berry, Valarie A. Zeithaml, and A. Parasuraman, "Five Imperatives for Improving Service Quality," *Sloan Management Review,* Summer 1990, p. 29; the fourth story is adapted from Andrew H. Malcolm, "For Police, a Delicate Job of Reordering Priorities," *New York Times,* October 28, 1990, p. 12.

2. Leonard L. Berry, "How To Sell New Services," *American Demographics,* October 1989, p. 42.

3. Valarie A. Zeithaml, "How Consumer Evaluation Processes Differ Between Goods and Services," in James H. Donnelly and William R. George, eds., *Marketing of Services* (Chicago: American Marketing Association, 1981), pp. 186–189.

4. James Brian Quinn, Thomas L. Doorley, and Penny C. Paquette, "Beyond Products: Services-Based Strategy," *Harvard Business Review,* March–April 1990, p. 60.

5. Valarie A. Zeithaml, A. Parasuraman, and Leonard L. Berry, *Delivering Quality Service: Balancing Customer Perceptions and Expectations* (New York: Free Press, 1990). See also Stephen W. Brown, Evert Gummesson, Bo Edvardsson, and Bengtove Gustavsson, *Service Quality: Multidisciplinary and Multinational Perspectives* (Lexington, Mass.: Lexington Books, 1991), for a recent collection of multidisciplinary and multinational articles on the topic of service quality.

Chapter 2
Doing the Service Right the First Time

1. Valarie A. Zeithaml, A. Parasuraman, and Leonard L. Berry, *Delivering Quality Service: Balancing Customer Perceptions and Expectations* (New York: Free Press, 1990).

2. Frederick F. Reichheld and W. Earl Sasser, Jr., "Zero Defections: Quality Comes to Services," *Harvard Business Review*, September–October 1990, pp. 105–111.

3. Amanda Bennett, "Many Consumers Expect Better Service—and Say They Are Willing to Pay for It," *Wall Street Journal*, November 12, 1990, p. B1.

4. James L. Heskett, W. Earl Sasser, Jr., and Christopher W. L. Hart, *Service Breakthroughs: Changing the Rules of the Game* (New York: Free Press, 1990).

5. Zeithaml, Parasuraman, and Berry, *Delivering Quality Service*, p. 6.

6. *Corning Total Quality Digest* (Corning, N.Y.: Corning, Inc.), Volume II, p. 2.

7. Quoted in John Holusha, "The Baldrige Badge of Courage—and Quality," *New York Times*, October 21, 1990.

8. G. Lynn Shostack, "Service Design in the Operating Environment," in William R. George and Claudia E. Marshall, eds., *Developing New Services* (Chicago: American Marketing Association, 1984), p. 35.

9. Leonard L. Berry, "How to Sell New Services," *American Demographics*, October 1989, pp. 42–43.

10. "The Zapping of Federal Express," *Newsweek*, October 13, 1986, p. 57.

11. G. Lynn Shostack and Jane Kingman-Brundage, "Service Design and Development," in Carole A. Congram and Margaret L. Friedman, eds., *Handbook of Services Marketing* (New York: American Management Association, 1990).

12. William R. George and Barbara E. Gibson, "Blueprinting—A Tool for Managing Quality in Service," in Stephen W. Brown, Evert Gummesson, Bo Edvardsson, and Bengtove Gustavsson, eds., *Service Quality: Multidisciplinary and Multinational Perspectives* (Lexington, Mass.: Lexington Books, 1991), pp. 73–91.

13. G. Lynn Shostack, "'Service Blueprints' Help to Iron Out System Design Flaws Before Front Liners Take the Fall," *The Service Edge*, July–August 1990, p. 8.

14. Valarie A. Zeithaml, A. Parasuraman, and Leonard L. Berry, "Problems and Strategies in Services Marketing," *Journal of Marketing*, Spring 1985, pp. 33–46.

15. "Improving Service Doesn't Always Require Big Investment," *The Service Edge,* July–August 1990, pp. 1–3.

16. Lawrence Schein, *The Road to Total Quality—Views of Industry Experts,* Research Bulletin No. 239 (New York: The Conference Board, 1990), p. 16.

17. Leonard L. Berry, A. Parasuraman, and Valarie A. Zeithaml, "The Service-Quality Puzzle," *Business Horizons,* September–October 1988, pp. 35–43.

18. David B. Luther, "Continuous Quality Improvement: The Ever-Widening Network," keynote address delivered at the Conference Board's Third Annual Quality Conference, New York, April 2, 1990.

19. "Hospital, Heal Thyself," *Business Week,* August 27, 1990, pp. 66–68.

Chapter 3
Doing the Service Very Right the Second Time

1. Christopher W. L. Hart, James L. Heskett, and W. Earl Sasser, Jr., "The Profitable Art of Service Recovery," *Harvard Business Review,* July–August 1990, p. 148. For an earlier article stressing the importance of service recovery, see Chip R. Bell and Ron Zemke, "Service Breakdown: The Road to Recovery," *Management Review,* October 1987.

2. A comprehensive discussion of this study can be found in Alan R. Andreasen and Arthur Best, "Consumers Complain—Does Business Respond?" *Harvard Business Review,* July–August 1977, pp. 93–101.

3. A comprehensive discussion of this study can be found in Valarie A. Zeithaml, A. Parasuraman, and Leonard L. Berry, *Delivering Quality Service: Balancing Customer Perceptions and Expectations* (New York: Free Press, 1990).

4. Andreasen and Best, "Consumers Complain," p. 101.

5. Quoted in "Improving Service Doesn't Always Require Big Investment," *The Service Edge,* July–August 1990, p. 3.

6. Hart, Heskett, and Sasser, "The Profitable Art of Service Recovery," p. 150.

7. See, for example, A. Parasuraman, "An Attributional Framework for Assessing the Perceived Value of a Service," in Carol Surprenant, ed., *Add Value to Your Service* (Chicago: American Marketing Association, 1988), pp. 21–24; and Carol F. Surprenant and Michael

R. Solomon, "Predictability and Personalization in the Service Encounter," *Journal of Marketing,* April 1987, pp. 86–96.

8. Patricia Sellers, "How to Handle Customers' Gripes," *Fortune,* October 24, 1988, pp. 88–100.

9. Mary Jo Bitner, Bernard M. Booms, and Mary Stanfield Tetreault, "The Service Encounter: Diagnosing Favorable and Unfavorable Incidents," *Journal of Marketing,* January 1990, pp. 71–84.

10. Jon Anton, "Why It Pays to Solicit Customer Complaints," *Telemarketing,* Vol. 7, No. 5, November 1988.

11. Ibid.

12. The Embassy Suites and Cadillac examples are both from Bro Uttal, "Companies That Serve You Best," *Fortune,* December 7, 1987, pp. 98–116.

13. Hart, Heskett, and Sasser, "The Profitable Art of Service Recovery," pp. 148–156.

14. More information on service blueprinting is given in Chapter 2.

15. A. Parasuraman, Leonard L. Berry, and Valarie A. Zeithaml, "Understanding Customer Expectations of Service," *Sloan Management Review,* Spring 1991, pp. 39–48.

16. Leonard L. Berry, A. Parasuraman, and Valarie A. Zeithaml, "The Service-Quality Puzzle," *Business Horizons,* September–October 1988, pp. 35–43.

17. Bitner, Booms, and Tetreault, "The Service Encounter."

18. Hart, Heskett, and Sasser, "The Profitable Art of Service Recovery," p. 155.

19. John A. Goodman, Arlene R. Malech, and Sonja Boyd, "Danger! Angry Customer!" *American Banking Journal,* January 1987, p. 66.

20. Hart, Heskett, and Sasser, "The Profitable Art of Service Recovery," pp. 148–156.

21. Mary C. Gilly, "Postcomplaint Processes: From Organizational Response to Repurchase Behavior," *The Journal of Consumer Affairs,* Winter 1987, pp. 293–313.

22. Quoted in "Federal Express Uses 3-Level Recovery System," *The Service Edge,* December 1990, p. 5.

23. Timothy W. Firnstahl, "My Employees Are My Service Guarantee," *Harvard Business Review,* July–August 1989, p. 29.

24. Leonard L. Berry, Valarie A. Zeithaml, and A. Parasuraman, "Five Imperatives for Improving Service Quality," *Sloan Management Review,* Summer 1990, pp. 29–38.

25. Sellers, "How to Handle Customers' Gripes."

26. Firnstahl, "My Employees Are My Service Guarantee," pp. 28–32.

27. Ibid., p. 30.

28. Sellers, "How to Handle Customers' Gripes."

29. S. C. Gwynne, "New Kid on the Dock," *Time,* September 17, 1990, pp. 62–63.

30. Firnstahl, "My Employees Are My Service Guarantee," p. 31.

31. John F. Yarbrough, "TARP Information Systems," *Salisbury* (Maryland) *Daily Times* (Business Section), August 18, 1990.

Chapter 4
Managing and Exceeding Customers' Expectations

1. Robert C. Lewis and Bernard H. Booms, "The Marketing Aspects of Service Quality," in Leonard L. Berry, G. Lynn Shostack, and Gregory Upah, eds., *Emerging Perspectives on Services Marketing* (Chicago: American Marketing Association, 1983), pp. 99–107; A. Parasuraman, Valarie A. Zeithaml, and Leonard L. Berry, "A Conceptual Model of Service Quality and Its Implications for Future Research," *Journal of Marketing,* Fall 1985, pp. 41–50.

2. One of the earlier writings on this subject is Christian Gronroos, *Strategic Management and Marketing in the Service Sector,* Helsinki: Swedish School of Economics and Business Administration, working paper, 1982.

3. See, for example, Ernest R. Cadotte, Robert B. Woodruff, and Roger L. Jenkins, "Expectations and Norms in Models of Consumer Satisfaction," *Journal of Marketing Research,* August 1987, pp. 305–314.

4. Additional details about our study can be found in A. Parasuraman, Leonard L. Berry, and Valarie A. Zeithaml, "Understanding Customer Expectations of Service," *Sloan Management Review,* Spring 1991, pp. 39–48; and Valarie A. Zeithaml, Leonard L. Berry, and A. Parasuraman, *The Nature and Determinants of Customer Expectations of Service,* Cambridge, Mass.: Marketing Science Institute, research monograph, 1991. Several sections of the chapter have been adapted from material in these two papers.

5. We defined these dimensions and discussed their relative importance to customers in Chapter 2. In Chapter 3 we discussed their roles in problem-resolution service.

6. A. Parasuraman, Valarie A. Zeithaml, and Leonard L. Berry, "SERVQUAL: A Multiple-Item Scale for Measuring Consumer Perceptions of Service Quality," *Journal of Retailing,* April 1988, pp. 35–48.

7. A. Parasuraman, Leonard L. Berry, and Valarie A. Zeithaml,

"Guidelines for Conducting Service Quality Research," *Marketing Research,* December 1990, pp. 34–44, offers general methodological suggestions for undertaking the types of research we recommend in this and the previous two chapters.

Chapter 5
Turning Marketing into a Line Function

1. Leonard L. Berry, "Big Ideas In Services Marketing," *Journal of Consumer Marketing,* Spring 1986, p. 47.
2. Barry I. Deutsch, "Marketers Must Resist the Urge to Say 'Yes Sir'," *American Banker,* February 25, 1988, p. 4.

Chapter 6
Managing the Evidence

1. G. Lynn Shostack, "The Sins of Alfred Sloan," a presentation to the Second International Quality in Services Conference, Norwalk, Connecticut, July 10, 1990.
2. Philip Kotler, "Atmospherics as a Marketing Tool," *Journal of Retailing,* Winter 1973–74, p. 50.
3. G. Lynn Shostack, "Breaking Free from Product Marketing," *Journal of Marketing,* April 1977, p. 78.
4. Leonard L. Berry, "Services Marketing Is Different," *Business,* May–June 1980, p. 26.
5. Gregory D. Upah and James W. Fulton, "Situation Creation in Service Marketing," in John A. Czepiel, Michael R. Solomon, and Carol F. Surprenant, eds. *The Service Encounter* (Lexington, Mass.: Lexington Books, 1985), p. 256.
6. Julie Baker, "The Role of the Environment in Marketing Services: The Consumer Perspective," in John A. Czepiel, Carole Congram, and James Shanahan, eds., *The Service Challenge: Integrating for Competitive Advantage* (Chicago: American Marketing Association, 1987), pp. 79–84.
7. Carl Sewell and Paul B. Brown, *Customers for Life* (New York: Doubleday Currency, 1990), chapters 22 and 24.
8. Ibid., p. 113.
9. Michael R. Solomon, "Packaging the Service Provider," *The Service Industries Journal,* March 1985, pp. 65 and 67.
10. William R. George and Leonard L. Berry, "Guidelines for the Advertising of Services," *Business Horizons,* July–August 1981, p. 53.

11. See Christopher W. L. Hart, "The Power of Unconditional Service Guarantees," *Harvard Business Review,* July–August 1988, pp. 54–62.

12. Ibid., p. 55.

13. See, for example, "Frank Lorenzo: The Final Days," *Business Week,* August 27, 1990, p. 33.

14. Maritz AmeriPoll, press release, August 15, 1990.

15. Upah and Fulton, "Situation Creation in Service Marketing," p. 260.

16. Francesca Turchiano, "The (Un)malling of America," *American Demographics,* April 1990, p. 38.

17. Mary Jo Bitner, "Consumer Responses to the Physical Environment in Service Settings," in M. Venkentesan, Diane Schmalensee, and Claudia Marshall, eds., *Creativity in Services Marketing: What's New, What Works, What's Developing* (Chicago: American Marketing Association, 1986), p. 90.

18. P. Anne van't Haaff, "Top Quality: A Way of Life," in *Distinguished Papers: Service Quality in the 1990s,* Panel Session, Sixth General Assembly, World Future Society, July 1989 (New York: St. John's University Business Research Institute, December 1989), pp. 10–11.

19. Sewell and Brown, *Customers for Life,* p. 116.

20. Mary Jo Bitner, "Evaluating Service Encounters: The Effects of Physical Surroundings and Employee Responses," *Journal of Marketing,* April 1990, pp. 69–82.

21. "Profiting from the Nonprofits," *Business Week,* March 26, 1990, pp. 66–74.

22. Patricia Leigh Brown, "Disney Deco," *New York Times Magazine,* April 8, 1990, pp. 18–22, 42–43, 48–49, 68.

23. Ibid., p. 42.

24. Julie Baker, Leonard L. Berry, and A. Parasuraman, "The Marketing Impact of Branch Facility Design," *Journal of Retail Banking,* Summer 1988, pp. 33–42.

25. Sewell and Brown, *Customers for Life,* p. 122.

26. Shostack, "The Sins of Alfred Sloan."

Chapter 7
Branding the Company

1. Chris Easingwood, "Service Design and Service Company Strategy," in Susan Jackson, John Bateson, Richard Chase, and Benjamin Schneider, eds., *Marketing, Operations and Human Resources In-*

sights into Services, Proceedings of the First International Research Seminar in Service Management, Université d'Aix-Marseille, France, 1990, pp. 188–199.

2. The discussion of the characteristics is based on Leonard L. Berry, Edwin F. Lefkowith, and Terry Clark, "In Services, What's in a Name?" *Harvard Business Review,* September–October 1988, pp. 28–30.

3. As quoted in John D. Marsh, "What's in a Bank Name? Profit," *The Southern Banker,* October 1989, p. 22.

4. Thomas J. Fitzgerald, "Understanding the Differences and Similarities Between Services and Products to Exploit Your Competitive Advantage," *The Journal of Business and Industrial Marketing,* Summer 1987, pp. 29–34.

Chapter 8
Marketing to Existing Customers

1. Michael J. O'Connor, "Most Failures Come in the Second Act; Retailing Is No Exception," *International Trends in Retailing,* Fall 1989, pp. 17–21.

2. Ibid., p. 21.

3. Frederick F. Reichheld and W. Earl Sasser, Jr., "Zero Defections: Quality Comes to Services," *Harvard Business Review,* September–October 1990, pp. 301–307.

4. Ibid.

5. See "Focus on Customer Retention is a Proven Profit Strategy," *The Service Edge,* June 1990, p. 2.

6. John A. Czepiel and Robert Gilmore, "Exploring the Concept of Loyalty in Services," in John A. Czepiel, Carole Congram, and James Shanahan, eds., *The Service Challenge: Integrating for Competitive Advantage* (Chicago: American Marketing Association, 1987), pp. 91–94.

7. Michael R. Solomon, Carol F. Surprenant, John A. Czepiel, and Evelyn G. Gutman, "A Role Theory Perspective on Dyadic Interactions: The Service Encounter," *Journal of Marketing,* Winter 1985, pp. 99–111.

8. A. Parasuraman, Leonard L. Berry, and Valarie A. Zeithaml, "Understanding Customer Expectations of Service," *Sloan Management Review,* Spring 1991, pp. 39–48.

9. Reichheld and Sasser, "Zero Defections," p. 302.

10. Lisa H. Towle, "Retailers Take a Tip from the Airlines," *New York Times,* December 3, 1989, p. F13.

11. Bridget O'Brian and Asra Q. Nomani, "American Lets Flyers Trade Miles," *Wall Street Journal*, April 4, 1990, p. B1.

12. F. J. Stephenson and J. Fox, "Corporate Attitudes Toward Frequent Flyer Programs," *Transportation Journal*, Fall 1987, pp. 10–22.

13. Terrence J. Kearney, "Frequent Flyer Programs: A Failure in Competitive Strategy, with Lessons for Management," *The Journal of Services Marketing*, Fall 1989, pp. 49–59.

14. James H. Donnelly, Jr., Leonard L. Berry, and Thomas W. Thompson, *Marketing Financial Services—A Strategic Vision*, (Homewood, Ill.: Dow Jones-Irwin, 1985), p. 113.

15. For an excellent discussion of the meaning of customer loyalty, see Czepiel and Gilmore, "Exploring the Concept of Loyalty in Services."

16. Lawrence A. Crosby, Kenneth R. Evans, and Deborah Cowles, "Relationship Quality in Services Selling: An Interpersonal Influence Perspective," *Journal of Marketing*, July 1990, pp. 68–81.

17. Chris Costanzo, "Doing Thy Will . . . and Thy Whim," *Western Banker*, March 1990.

18. Peter W. Turnbull and David T. Wilson, "Developing and Protecting Profitable Customer Relationships," *Industrial Marketing Management*, August 1989, p. 237.

19. Tom Peters, "Twenty Propositions about Service," a speech to the International Customer Service Association, Phoenix, Arizona, September 20, 1988.

20. Leonard L. Berry, "Relationship Marketing," in Leonard L. Berry, G. Lynn Shostack, and Gregory D. Upah, eds., *Emerging Perspectives on Services Marketing* (Chicago: American Marketing Association, 1983), p. 26.

21. For an excellent discussion of the construct of value, see Valarie A. Zeithaml, "Consumer Perceptions of Price, Quality, and Value: A Means-End Model and Synthesis of Evidence," *Journal of Marketing*, July 1988, pp. 2–22.

22. Parasuraman, Berry, and Zeithaml, "Understanding Customer Expectations of Service."

23. Ron Zemke, "The Operations Era," *The Service Edge*, June 1990, p. 6.

24. As quoted by Ron Zemke, ibid.

25. Parasuraman, Berry, and Zeithaml, "Understanding Customer Expectations of Service."

26. Leonard L. Berry and Thomas W. Thompson, "Relationship Banking Keeps Clients Returning," *Trusts & Estates*, November 1985, p. 29.

27. Reichheld and Sasser, "Zero Defections," p. 304.

28. Parasuraman, Berry, and Zeithaml, "Understanding Customer Expectations of Service."

29. Patricia Sellers, "What Customers Really Want," *Fortune,* June 4, 1990, p. 62.

30. Leonard L. Berry and Larry G. Gresham, "Relationship Retailing: Transforming Customers into Clients," *Business Horizons,* November–December 1986, p. 45.

Chapter 9
Marketing to Employees

1. As quoted in Carole A. Congram, John A. Czepiel, and James B. Shanahan, "Achieving Internal Integration in Service Organizations: Five Propositions," in John A. Czepiel, Carole A. Congram, and James B. Shanahan, eds., *The Service Challenge: Integrating for Competitive Advantage* (Chicago: American Marketing Association, 1987), p. 5.

2. A. Parasuraman, Leonard L. Berry, and Valarie Zeithaml, "An Empirical Examination of Relationships in an Extended Service Quality Model," *Marketing Science Institute Research Program Series,* December 1990, Report No. 90-122.

3. Leonard L. Berry, Valarie A. Zeithaml, and A. Parasuraman, "Five Imperatives for Improving Service Quality," *Sloan Management Review,* Summer 1990, p. 31.

4. Valarie A. Zeithaml, A. Parasuraman, and Leonard L. Berry, *Delivering Quality Service: Balancing Customer Perceptions and Expectations* (New York: Free Press, 1990), p. 164.

5. Ibid.

6. Roger Selbert, "The Educational Future," *FutureScan,* September 12, 1988, p. 1.

7. Amanda Bennett, "As Pool of Skilled Help Tightens, Firms Move to Broaden Their Role," *Wall Street Journal,* May 8, 1989, p. A6.

8. Carl Sewell and Paul B. Brown, *Customers for Life* (New York: Doubleday Currency, 1990), p. 68.

9. Leonard L. Berry, David R. Bennett, and Carter W. Brown, *Service Quality: A Profit Strategy for Financial Institutions* (Homewood, Ill.: Dow Jones-Irwin, 1989), p. 51.

10. Roger Selbert, "Dealing with the Worker Shortage," *FutureScan,* September 18, 1989, p. 2.

11. Von Johnston, "How to Attract and Keep the Best Employees," a

presentation to the Texas A&M University Center for Retailing Studies Symposium, San Antonio, Texas, November 1, 1990.

12. Kathleen S. Alexander, "How to Think About the People Issues for the Nineties," a presentation to the Texas A&M University Center for Retailing Studies Symposium, San Antonio, Texas, November 1, 1990.

13. Joel Dreyfuss, "Get Ready for the New Work Force," *Fortune,* April 23, 1990, pp. 172, 176.

14. Alexander, "How to Think About the People Issues."

15. Bruce G. Posner, "Taming the Labor Shortage," *Inc.,* November 1989, p. 168.

16. Jeffrey S. Wells, "How to Manage Organizational Change When Expanding," a presentation to the Texas A&M University Center for Retailing Studies Symposium, San Antonio, Texas, November 2, 1990.

17. James L. Heskett, "Lessons in the Service Sector," *Harvard Business Review,* March–April 1987, p. 121.

18. Tim W. Ferguson, "Inspired from Above, ServiceMaster Dignifies Those Below," *Wall Street Journal,* May 8, 1990, p. A21.

19. Timothy W. Firnstahl, "My Employees Are My Service Guarantee," *Harvard Business Review,* July–August, 1989, pp. 28–29.

20. As quoted in Dave Zielinski, "Effective Service Messages are Sent Often—and at All Job Levels," *The Service Edge,* May 1990, p. 3.

21. Zeithaml, Parasuraman, and Berry, *Delivering Quality Service,* pp. 154–155.

22. Berry, Bennett, and Brown, *Service Quality,* p. 160.

23. Wendy Leebov, "Many Middle Managers Require a Mindset Change to Facilitate Service Improvement," *The Service Edge,* May 1990, p. 8.

24. Posner, "Taming the Labor Shortage," p. 168.

25. Christopher W. Hart, "Internal Guarantees: JIT Equivalent for Services," unpublished working paper.

26. Berry, Bennett, and Brown, *Service Quality,* p. 161.

27. This paragraph and several others in the present and following sections are based on Berry, Zeithaml, and Parasuraman, "Five Imperatives for Improving Service Quality," pp. 29–38.

28. "People in Organizations," *The Royal Bank Letter,* November–December 1989, p. 4.

29. Parasuraman, Berry, and Zeithaml, "An Empirical Examination of Relationships."

30. As quoted in Brian Dumaine, "Who Needs a Boss," *Fortune,* May 7, 1990, p. 53.

31. See "Work Teams Can Rev Up Paper-Pushers, Too," *Business Week,* November 28, 1988, pp. 64–72.

32. As quoted in Dumaine, "Who Needs a Boss," p. 60.

33. Berry, Bennett, and Brown, *Service Quality,* pp. 138–139.

34. Lowell Mayone, "How to Improve Human Performance in Retailing," a presentation to the Texas A&M University Center for Retailing Studies Symposium, San Antonio, Texas, November 2, 1990.

35. George A. Rieder, "Incentives That Work: Rewarding Performance and Commitment," a presentation to the Mellon Bank Conference for CEOs, Scottsdale, Arizona, March 7, 1990.

36. Fred Luthans and Tim R. V. Davis, "Applying Behavioral Management Techniques in Service Organizations," in David E. Bowen, Richard B. Chase, Thomas G. Cummings, and associates, eds., *Service Management Effectiveness—Balancing Strategy, Organization and Human Resources, Operations, and Marketing* (San Francisco: Jossey-Bass, 1990), p. 206.

37. Linda Cooper and Beth Summers, *Getting Started in Quality* (Chicago: The First National Bank of Chicago, 1990), p. 14.

38. Claudia H. Deutsch, "Asking Workers What They Think," *New York Times,* April 22, 1990, Business Section.

Chapter 10
Services Marketing in the Nineties

1. Mary Jo Bitner, Bernard M. Booms, and Mary Stanfield Tetreault, "The Service Encounter: Diagnosing Favorable and Unfavorable Incidents," *Journal of Marketing,* January 1990, pp. 71–84.

2. James Brian Quinn and Penny C. Paquette, "Technology in Services: Creating Organizational Revolutions," *Sloan Management Review,* Winter 1990, p. 76.

3. David B. Luther, Larry Bankowski, and others, "Continuous Quality Improvement: The Ever-Widening Network," a presentation to the Conference Board Quality Conference, New York City, April 2, 1990.

4. The information in this paragraph is based on remarks by John Pepper, President of Procter & Gamble, at the Xerox Quality Forum II, Leesburg, Virginia, August 2, 1990.

5. Max D. Hopper, "Rattling SABRE—New Ways to Compete on Information," *Harvard Business Review,* May–June 1990, pp. 123–124.

6. Lou Grabowsky, "Globalization: Reshaping the Retail Marketplace," *Arthur Andersen Retailing Issues Letter,* November 1989, p. 2.

7. Ibid., p. 4.

8. "Federal Express's Fred Smith," *Inc.,* October 1986, pp. 46–47.

9. Carolyn Burstein, "Service Quality in the Federal Government," a presentation to the Second International Quality in Services Conference, July 10, 1990, Norwalk, Connecticut.

10. Carol F. Surprenant and Michael R. Solomon, "Predictability and Personalization in the Service Encounter," *Journal of Marketing,* April 1987, pp. 86–96.

11. Cynthia Crossen, "Customers at Mercy of Delivery Services," *Wall Street Journal,* March 29, 1990, p. B4.

12. Paul B. Brown, "The Real Cost of Customer Service," *Inc.,* September 1990, p. 60.

13. Roger Selbert, "The Strategic Alliance of the Future: Info Management and Front-Line End Users," *FutureScan,* October 16, 1989, pp. 2–4.

14. Quinn and Paquette, "Technology in Services," pp. 67–78.

15. Hopper, "Rattling SABRE," p. 122.

16. "One Million Shoppers Eye Interactive DIY Info Kiosk," *Inside Retailing,* May 7, 1990, p. 3.

17. Paul B. Carroll, "Computers Cut Through the Service Maze," *Wall Street Journal,* May 1, 1990, p. B1.

18. Andrew H. Malcom, "For Police, a Delicate Job of Reordering Priorities," *New York Times,* October 28, 1990, p. 12.

19. Bickley Townsend, "Hotels of the Future—An Interview with Adam M. Aron," *American Demographics,* January 1990, p. 47.

20. Eben Shapiro, "A Drugstore Industry Leader Raises the Level of Its Game," *New York Times,* August 26, 1990, p. 16.

21. John Schneidawind, "Xerox's New Copier Calls for Repairs Before You Do," *USA Today,* March 28, 1990, p. 7B.

22. As quoted in "Xerox Corp. and Milliken & Co. are this Year's Winners of the Malcolm Baldrige National Quality Award," *The Service Edge,* December 1989, p. 5.

23. Luther et al., "Continuous Quality Improvement."

24. Lawrence A. Crosby, "A Normative Framework for Total Quality Information Integration," in Susan Jackson, John Bateson, Richard Chase, and Benjamin Schneider, eds., *Marketing, Operations and Human Resources Insights into Services,* Proceedings of the First International Research Seminar in Service Management, Université d'Aix-Marseille, France, 1990, pp. 112–132.

Index

CPSIA information can be obtained at www.ICGtesting.com
Printed in the USA
LVOW11s1337080116

469835LV00001B/159/P